Power^{ed} Play

Power^{ed} Play

Because Who Really Wants to *Work* on Relationships?

Gail A. W. Silverstein

LEON SMITH
PUBLISHING

Copyright © 2021 Gail A. W. Silverstein

All rights reserved. No part of this book may be reproduced or transmitted in any form or by any means without written permission of the publisher, except in the case of brief quotations embodied in critical articles and reviews.

This material has been written and published solely for educational purposes. The author and the publisher shall have neither liability nor responsibility to any person or entity with respect to any loss, damage, or injury caused or alleged to be caused directly or indirectly by the information contained in this book.

Statements made and opinions expressed in this publication are those of the author and do not necessarily reflect the views of the publisher or indicate an endorsement by the publisher.

ISBN: 978-1-945446-96-2

Applauding Powered Play

"Gail White-Silverstein has devised a unique set of games that people who desire to improve the quality of their relationships can play to both know themselves as well as the other person(s). The games are revealing and empowering for the participants as well as fun. Given that humans like to play games, these games are not based on winners and losers but on mutual benefits as well as intimacy and quality. A breath of fresh air for relationships other than just talking about it."

— Terry Cole-Whittaker, DD
Founder of Terry Cole-Whittaker Ministries
United Church of Religious Science Minister
New Thought Writer
Author of Six International Bestselling Books, including
What You Think of Me Is None of My Business
terrycolewhittaker.com

*I dedicate this book to my family
who constantly challenge me to do better.
You are my perfect family.*

Table of Contents

Acknowledgments   11
Introduction to Power^{ed} Games   13

CHAPTER ONE
  Let's Play Naked: Truth or Dare   15
    Naked Basketball!   26
    Double Dare   47
    Triple Dare   50
    Don't I Know You?   52

CHAPTER TWO
  I've Met My Match: My Perfect Match   55
    Perfect Strangers   60
    Naked Tic-Tac-Toe   62

CHAPTER THREE
  Dance Class: Remember Your Backpack   69
    Perfect Strangers (Level 2)   78
    Don't I Know You? (Level 2)   80

CHAPTER FOUR
  The Feminine Fuse: Inspire Higher   83
    Love Your Pet   89
    Your Perfect Pet   92

CHAPTER FIVE
  Time-Out: Good and Bad Arguments   95
    Can You Hear Me Now?   103
    Do I Know You?   107

CHAPTER SIX
    Show and Tell: Sex Conversations   111
        Bedtime Stories   117
        Private Monologues   121

CHAPTER SEVEN
    My Favorite Playmate: Laughter Is Romantic   125
        You Gotta Laugh!   131
        That's Funny!   135

CHAPTER EIGHT
    MC^2: Relationship Energy   137
        Two Naked People: Couples STRIP   144
        Your Power^{ed} Couple Play   147
        Your Power^{ed} Relationship Play   149

About the Author   153

Acknowledgments

Rev. Terry Cole-Whittaker:
Where would I be without your Spiritual Mastery Course and your coaching? What a blessing you are to my life.

Dr. Rev. Michael Beckwith:
My minister and spiritual coach. God, I'm glad you said yes over thirty years ago! I can't imagine my life without you and these teachings.

Rev. Coco Stewart:
Ah! It's finally done! Words cannot adequately describe my respect, admiration, and love for you! This book would not be so without you.

Eisha Mason:
Thank you, thank you, thank you for your support, encouragement, friendship, and example! I love you, my sister.

My husband, David:
Wow, have you taught me a lot about relationships! You are my perfect match! I love you.

My daughter, Love:
You inspire me and teach me. I love you.

My son, Chris,
You compel me and teach me. I love you.

Introduction to Power^ed Games

Eric is frustrated. He's meeting up with an old friend and is running late. He picks up his cell phone to say he's on his way. His phone's dead. "@#&$!"

Kim loves her new camera; it takes great pictures. Today is her sister's surprise birthday party, and Kim is the designated photographer. She's ready. When Kim's sister walks in, her sister is completely surprised. Perfect! Kim tries to take the picture, but nothing happens. The camera is dead.

Nate had a rough day. He can't wait to get home and relax with his wife, Laura. When he walks in the door, Laura barely looks at him. Laura's had a rough day too. Nate's battery is drained and so is Laura's. Nate musters up a cold stare, and Laura returns the sentiment.

Aaron and Gina connected several months ago. In the beginning, it was long phone conversations, hot dates, and fun weekends. During one of their recent conversations, Aaron made some comments that really bothered Gina, but she didn't say anything about it. Aaron notices Gina is acting funny since their last phone call. But when he asks her if something is wrong, she says no. They both begin to wonder: *Are we really connected?*

Whether we've been married for a while, just started a relationship, or are looking for the right connection, sometimes we need a recharge. We can all benefit from activities that *power* us and our partner, or *power* us for our right relationship. But who wants to spend hours working at relationship? We'd like it to be as easy as plugging our phone into a charger, but unfortunately, that is not going to happen.

But, what if it were playful or fun?

Power^{ed} Play games provide an opportunity to have fun while gaining a new perspective on our relationship and ourselves, or even learning something new. These games are about how to reveal and share what powers us in our intimate relationships and how to escape the distractions that often interfere with what we think, what we want, or what we do. Whether you're in a short-term or long-term relationship, married, casually dating, thirty-something or fifty-something, heterosexual or homosexual, I've found you don't need a list of rules to follow to improve your relationship. Nor do you need to do what another couple does.

We need to develop deeper and truer connections that recharge us and our relationships. Also, it's likely that how we do or don't connect with a significant other will be reflected in how we do or don't connect in our other relationships, so you will also find games to help you improve your other relationships as well.

When we are power^{ed}, not only do we power our partner, we power our families, our friends, our communities, and beyond.

Adult Games

Each chapter has one or more games, and each game is rated:

- Games rated MC are for couples who are *married* or in a *committed* relationship.

- Games rated S are for *singles* who want to be in a relationship. Those with S^2 are for anyone who wants to generally improve their relationship with someone else.

These games are fun ways to energize you and your relationship. If you are married or in a committed relationship and your partner is not available to read this book with you, the games are an easy way to get them involved without making them read the book.

Ready to play?

Chapter One

Let's Play Naked: Truth or Dare

Truth is sexy? Yes. In the same way lying naked in the arms of a lover can ignite our deepest passions and senses, so, too, can sharing our raw, honest truth. There is something fundamentally sensual about baring our nakedness.

In its most primitive form, truth may erupt from an emotionally charged argument in which resentments, secrets, and insecurities are exposed. I refer to these as *truth surges*—often followed by apologies, promises . . . and make-up sex.

But does raw truth only emerge from an emotionally charged argument? No. An uninhibited heart anchored in truth can be quite alluring and seductive. We humans are intrigued by another's inhibitions. But it's a curious dance because we also desire acceptance of our own. Being able to stand in our own truth, while acknowledging and accepting the truth of another, requires courage, clarity, passion, and resilience.

Think back to a time when you were firmly grounded in your own truth with no hidden agendas, no intent to manipulate, no arrogance—just a solid commitment to your truth.

How did you feel? How did others respond?

Did you capture your listener's attention? Perhaps you formed a bond with those who agreed with you. Perhaps you gained the respect of those who disagreed with you. You likely experienced a sense of inner satisfaction because you remained true to who you were. And while a persuasive speech may capture an audience's attention, a well-crafted argument does not invoke the inspiration and respect that clear words of conviction can.

But what *truth* am I talking about?

Naked Truth

There are different types of truths. For example, there are *absolute* truths, such as physical laws. These are regarded as facts and proven through scientific methodologies. These are truths that are always true. Examples are aerodynamics and gravity.

Then, there are what I consider *principle* truths, which are more subjective. Principle truths relate to general beliefs and values and tend to join individuals who share that same principle truth. Belief in a democracy, belief in God and how to practice that belief, and educational standards are examples of principle truths.

Beyond principle truths are what I call *core* truths. Core truths are at the core of who we are. Like principle truths, these truths are subjective—they are conceptual and intangible. They can certainty be related to principle truths. Additionally, although core truths evolve or may become distorted by stress or fear, they are like absolute truths in that they are always present in us in one form or another; they are what we believe, what we value, an integral part of who we are, and are at the root of how we connect with others. To put it another way, CORE truths *Create Our Relationship Energy*. Additionally, our CORE truth impacts our relationship with our family, friends, strangers, even our circumstances and ourselves—and, of course, our significant other. In this playful exploration of power[ed] relationships, we are looking at what happens when individuals express and share their CORE truths.

But, before we can express our CORE truths, we must know them. And to know our CORE truths, we must shed our masks, our pretenses, our defense mechanisms, our emotions, and our ego—we must *get naked*. In this context, our CORE truths are our complete nakedness. They are the fundamental nature of who we are without trying to get something back. They are the beliefs and values at the core of who we are. When individuals connect based on their CORE truths, a bond forms.

> **Undressing Jane – Part 1**
>
> There's a woman we'll call Jane who shied away from people when she was a child. Hurtful childhood experiences made Jane feel uneasy around other people. As a chubby little girl who grew up as an only child, Jane felt awkward. She had parents and family who loved her, but who were sometimes challenged by how to show it. At times, Jane felt isolated, inadequate, and unattractive, with her early teen years being the toughest.
>
> At nineteen years old, Jane left her parents' house, then married her college boyfriend. In her early twenties, she had two beautiful children, was active in her church, continued her college education, and she and her husband purchased their first house. But, by her late twenties, her marriage was in trouble, she and her husband filed bankruptcy, she discontinued school, and she began working full time. She also began to have grand mal seizures.
>
> In her early thirties, within a span of five years, Jane lost her mother to cancer, suddenly lost her father, struggled through a messy divorce, was expelled from her church, and moved twice—

all while caring for her two children and maintaining a job during a tough recession. All these situations forced Jane to repeatedly search deep inside herself—sometimes, nearer and nearer to her breaking point. She was depressed, insecure, didn't trust others, was stubborn, and sometimes talked about giving up on life completely. But she had two children who depended on her. She did believe in a Higher Power, although she was not always clear how that Power impacted her life. Jane didn't have the answers about how to change her situation—neither did friends or family. So, she was forced to search for them herself.

She quickly learned there was no one place to find answers. She studied books about ancient philosophies, nature, the body, and the universe. She attended places of worship, Al-Anon meetings, personal growth seminars, she meditated, and she prayed. She sought assistance from therapists, personal growth coaches, and spiritual teachers. She took whatever resonated with her from each experience, encounter, and resource and let go of what didn't.

Through the anger, confusion, and pain, Jane uncovered what was creating her experiences. She saw how she was allowing her masks, defense mechanisms, and fears to define her. She started recognizing she wasn't defined by what others said unless she allowed it. She let go of limiting stories about who she was and what happened to her, and shifted how she saw herself, how she saw her life, and how she saw others. On this journey, she saw herself evolve. Insecurity became self-evaluation. Not trusting others evolved into trusting herself. Stubbornness became relentlessness.

By her early forties, Jane had established her own business, attained a comfortable income, enjoyed international travel, excellent health, and financial independence. Jane liked how she looked naked.

Core Connection

Whether it's a social movement or a playoff game, a sense of unity forms when individuals share similar ideas or beliefs. Something is ignited within us. This something transcends logic and reasoning and taps into the core of who we are. Therefore, it is no accident that this dynamic energy pulls individuals closer together. In some circumstances, individuals lose themselves to that which is greater than themselves.

So, what does all this have to do with being a couple or in a relationship?

If we want to be a powered couple—an energized couple— or have a power^{ed} relationship, we must develop a relationship in which both people feel their CORE truths are appreciated and respected. When two people know and share their CORE truths, their connection deepens. When two people either don't know their CORE truths or don't share their CORE truths, their connection weakens. But we need to make a few distinctions.

Again, we need to distinguish our CORE truths from our emotions, our opinions, our physical appearance, or our physical abilities. We respond with our emotions, we develop opinions, and we exhibit certain physical characteristics and abilities—but these are not at the core of who we are. Often these are formed around our CORE truths, as well as influenced by our experiences and environment. Additionally, we need to distinguish CORE truths from fears or insecurities that distort our CORE truths, or even worse, pretend to be our CORE truths. Our fears are very real to us, but these fears undermine and distort our CORE truths. And of course, secrets or big egos erode any attempts of being authentic. Consequently, pseudo-truths disrupt our relationship energy. Pseudo-truths create pseudo connections.

Remember Laura and Nate from the introduction? Why are they drained? Because they can't see each other beyond the challenges of the day. Instead, they see another person who needs something from them or they need something from. But what if they were aware of each other's CORE truths in this moment? What if Laura knew how important reliability was to Nate and that he was feeling inadequate because he was falling short? What if Nate knew how important having stability was to Laura and that she was scared because she felt completely overwhelmed and out of control? And what if they recognized their own CORE truths in this moment and could share their fears or even their secrets instead of cold stares?

And what about Aaron and Gina? Remember the phone conversation that left them both questioning their connection? They're questioning if they are really connected but for different reasons—reasons that could be related to their CORE truths—but most likely are related to their fears or pseudo-truths. Up to that point, Aaron always asked Gina what she liked and what she wanted to do before making plans, which Gina loved, of course. But in their last conversation, Aaron showed no interest in doing what Gina wanted. In fact, he mentioned other plans that didn't include her. This left Gina agitated and Aaron confused by her agitation. Gina didn't want things to change, and Aaron felt it was time for a change. Up to this point, Gina felt Aaron cared about her, but now she felt unimportant to him. Up to this point, Aaron was okay with doing what Gina wanted, but now he felt he needed to focus on what he wanted. And, just like that, assumptions were made and conclusions drawn.

To be a couple in which each person feels appreciated and respected for who they are, both people need to know and accept who the other person truly is. They need to know more than the other person's favorite food or color or favorite movie of all time. They need to know the other person's CORE truths—the truths that Create Our Relationship Energy. And of course, they each need to know their own.

When we know our CORE truths and share them with someone close to us, deep connections can develop. But what if individuals seem to have opposite CORE truths—one enjoys free-thinking while the other values discipline and rules? Do opposites really attract? Well, it's not so much whether individuals share the same CORE truths or not, but rather if they accept and respect each other's CORE truths. While having common CORE truths is likely to create a strong bond, standing in our own truths and allowing our significant other to do the same—without judgment or need to control—can be extremely sexy and create a strong unconditional bond. When there are no hidden agendas, and we set aside our egos and fears, and we acknowledge and understand our CORE truths, we are completely naked. And when we are naked, we are more likely to accept our partner—or potential partner—naked. When two people connect at this level of nakedness, they create a true connection.

Undressing Jane – Part 2

By her mid-forties, Jane retired from the corporate world and purchased a small business. Her life was purposeful and exciting, and her social life was often full but sometimes not fulfilling. She had to admit something was still not right. It was time to strip down even more. Jane needed to give up her stories regarding intimate relationships.

Jane let go of how she imagined her intimate relationship should be and opened herself up to what resonated with her deeper CORE truths. She began to pay more attention to her own internal messages. Within two weeks, unbeknownst to her, Mr. Right for Jane showed up. Jane didn't know he was Mr. Right for Jane at first, but she did recognize a deep connection with him. Later, Jane married him.

> Today, Jane manages her business, shares a beautiful home with *Mr. Right for Jane*, enjoys her family and wonderful friends, is active in her spiritual community, and truly loves helping others—and, yes, Jane is me. And I've never looked better naked.

Beyond Skin Deep

To get to our CORE truths, we must go deep inside, under the surface. We must shed our fears, ego, insecurities, or any other pseudo-truths. We must go beyond the people or things we value to discover the underlying CORE truth they represent.

Ever notice the insatiable curiosity of children? These inquisitive young minds can drive parents crazy with their unending questions. If you answer their question, they follow it up with another question. They may go four or five rounds before their curiosity is satisfied. Going below the surface can be a little complex, so you may need your childlike curiosity to get there.

For example, let's say I describe myself as a happy person. Why do I consider myself happy? What about my life makes me happy, or what's the source of my happiness? What if I describe myself as an angry person? What is behind my anger? What circumstance or person makes me angry and why? How about, "I am a caring person"? Why do I care? Whom do I care about? These descriptions may be true about us, but we're looking for what's underneath. That's where our CORE truths or CORE pseudo-truths can be found.

When digging deeper, the importance of money may show up for some. I am not here to debate this as a moral issue. But look beyond money and uncover what the money represents or how it makes you feel. That's where CORE truths or pseudo-truths are.

When we go deep, we uncover the truths or pseudo-truths that Create Our Relationship Energy. Our CORE truth connections allow us to connect deeper and our relationships are power^{ed}. CORE pseudo-truths connect us at a superficial level, at best, leaving our relationship vulnerable to frequent power outages. CORE pseudo-truths create pseudo-true connections.

Instant Messengers

First, are you on automatic? Are you rushing around and impatient because everyone around you is rushing and impatient? Are you being programmed by your environment? Our friends, family, workplace, social norms, social dynamics—even our digital environment—influence us. And sometimes, we need to stop for a moment and check if our actions are disconnected from our CORE truths—once we know what our CORE truths are. We live in a complex, information-driven society in which we are inundated with others' opinions and beliefs about what our opinions and beliefs should be. This is so commonplace, we may not notice how much we are influenced. It is virtually impossible for us to escape the plethora of ideas, opinions, and beliefs communicated to us through websites, email, social media, television shows, movies, music, magazines, books, and even commercials and billboards. These sources offer us entertainment, social connections, and useful information from which we make life decisions. But do we consider whose ideas, opinions, and beliefs we are receiving or—more importantly—how they are influencing our perspective about ourselves and those around us?

If we stop for a moment, we may be surprised by how much these persistent messengers impact what we believe, what we think is important, and what we feel about ourselves. While there may be nothing wrong with embracing ideas from these sources, it's important that we don't go on automatic. Turn off auto-mode.

Second, key people in our lives can embed ideas or attitudes in us based on our interaction with them. We can carry around that idea or attitude, but it really belongs to someone else. If these ideas and attitudes are good for us and we wish to embrace them—no problem. But sometimes, they are not so good for us. At other times, there is nothing wrong with them, but we may not choose to embrace them. Embedded ideas and attitudes can extend to how we see ourselves, what we feel is important, and how we see our partner.

Third, face it, everything that is true about us is not always desirable. We all have some ideas and attitudes that look better covered up. But when we get naked, we don't cover them up—we expose them and look at them. Maybe we have a need to be right. Intellectually, we know that no one can always be right, but we feel uneasy if it appears we are wrong about something. So, we never like to admit we are wrong.

But why? If we know that no one can be right all the time, then why do we have a problem admitting when we are wrong? It's likely we have a CORE truth that is distorted by fear, insecurity, or stress—again, pseudo-truths. But if we resolve our stress or fear, we can begin to uncover our CORE truth—which, by the way, will probably have nothing to do with being right.

Who we are changes over time. Who we are at five years old, compared to twenty-five years old, compared to forty-five years old, is different. However, our CORE truths tend to remain fairly consistent. Even under extreme circumstances, our CORE truths are likely to remain. If they are not distorted by fears, extreme circumstances can reveal our CORE truths even more. Consider how some people respond more effectively under pressure. Just when they think they've reached their limit, they surprise themselves and go beyond. You may be one of those people. In such instances, they are, no doubt, accessing hidden CORE truths—an important quality to share with a partner, particularly in a crisis.

Let's Get Naked!

Whether we're already married, in a committed relationship, or ready for our right relationship, sharing our CORE truths can be challenging. There are so many messengers vying for our attention, we can lose ourselves in the frenzy. Additionally, in a society that accepts stress as a part of daily living, we can certainly forget our CORE truths. Therefore, most of us can use a little help getting completely naked. So, let's play our first game, *Naked Basketball*!

GAME

NAKED BASKETBALL!

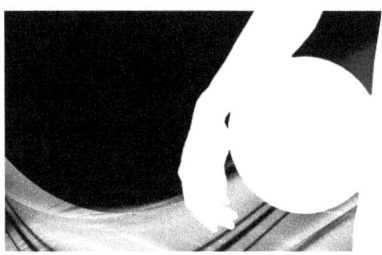

Imagine life is a team sport and those closest to you are your teammates or coaches. In this first game, we're going to imagine we're playing a team sport. Since I love basketball, the sport is basketball—I know you may favor another sport. But unlike any typical basketball game you've ever watched or played, we're getting naked in this one.

In basketball, as in many sports, teammates play their specific positions. Some play hard and contribute to the game while some play like they are the only one in the game who matters. Some teammates we get along with, while others we wish were on someone else's team. Additionally, coaches support and instruct us to shift our games. Skilled coaches help us perfect our game while unskilled coaches can throw our game off. In our games, sometimes we're on the floor and sometimes we're on the bench; sometimes we shoot a three-pointer and sometimes we assist; sometimes we're unstoppable and sometimes we're limping to the locker room.

Rated: MC and S²
Game Rules

Object
For you to strip down and get completely naked.

Set Up
This game is played by one player.

Those married or in a committed relationship: If you're married or in a committed relationship, you each play this game, but separately. If your partner is apprehensive about playing this game, you play the game first, then share your results with your partner. This may spark some interest. If not, as you play each game in this book, continue to invite your partner to play with you. *Naked Basketball!* is an important game as it is the foundation for other games.

Other games in this book may interest your partner. Mention some of the other games to your partner they may find interesting. For example, mention *Bedtime Stories*.

If your partner needs help playing this game, limit your assistance to clarifying how the game is played. Do not play the game for them.

Getting Started
You need to determine your team name. Think of a name that reflects how you see yourself or how you want to be seen. Once you have it, using the basketball court diagram below, write it down.

Next, identify your team members by reflecting on people in your life. Consider those who affect you. Take whatever time you need, even a day or two if necessary, and observe who impacts how you feel or think. To get the most out of this game, it is necessary to be clear and be honest.

Note: When filling in your team members' names, consider writing their names near the spots that best represent their position in your game, particularly, separating your starting lineup from the bench. Also, it is okay to have two or three players in your starting lineup and two or three on the bench. It is not necessary to have 5 players in your starting lineup or a full bench to play Naked Basketball. And remember, you can always come back and make changes as needed.

Here are some likely candidates:

- *Parents:* mother or mother figures, father or father figures
- *Siblings:* brothers or brother figures, sisters or sister figures
- *Relatives:* grandmothers, grandfathers, aunts, uncles, cousins
- *Intimate Relationships:* spouse or significant others, boyfriends, girlfriends
- *Peers:* friends, coworkers, colleagues, fellow students
- *Authoritative Relationships:* bosses, teachers, ministers, coaches
- *Subordinate Relationships:* children, nieces, nephews, students, employees
- *Instant Messengers:* social media, television, radio or talk shows, movies, publications, public speakers, work environment, socioeconomic class, and so on

The _____
(Write your team name here)

Note: When filling in your team members' names, consider writing their names near the spots that best represent their position in your game.

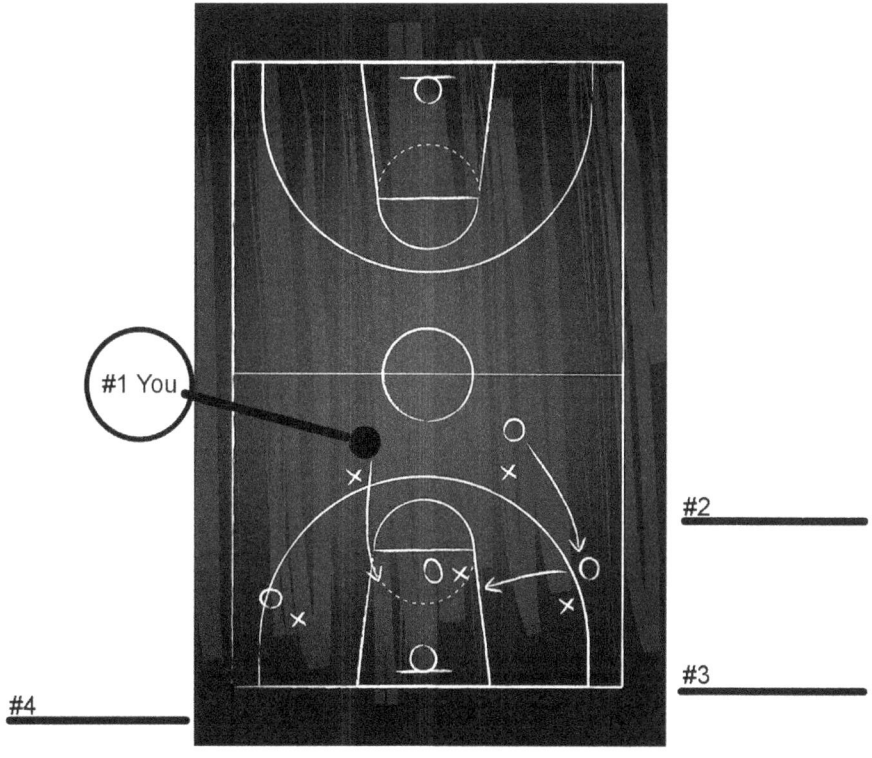

The Bench

_____

_____

_____

_____

_____

_____

Next, everyone wants to know what kind of player you are, particularly your team. They want to know what you'll bring to your games. They need to know your strengths and your weaknesses so they can assist you where you're weak and move out of your way where you're strong. So, using the Personal Bio sheet below, describe three to five qualities, talents, and traits you bring to your games.

Personal Bio

I am the type of player who:

(1) _____

(2) _____

(3) _____

(4) _____

(5) _____

Now, are you ready for the press? Often before a game, the team is interviewed by the press, particularly its star player, which, of course, is you. However, this interview process will be a little different. No one is going to call up your team members and start questioning them about you. Instead, you're going to reflect on what they have already told you or made you feel about yourself.

When you're ready, copy the name of your first team member from your game diagram onto your Press Interviews sheet. Now, take a moment and reflect on what that person has said about the type of player you are. What things have they said about you? Have they said you're persistent? Supportive? Maybe a little selfish? Next, do this for every team member on your team.

For Instant Messengers, reflect on how the message makes you feel. When you watch your favorite television show or engage in your favorite social media banter, does it make you feel smart? Lighthearted? Sexy? Connected? Write down one or two of these. And don't limit your descriptions to only compliments or criticism. Include what your team members have said or make you feel—good and not so good.

Also, refrain from statements like *good player* or *bad player*. Think more about the qualities, talents, abilities, habits, and characteristics the person has said make you a good or bad player.

Press Interviews

1) _____ said/or made me feel I am:

    (a)_____

    (b)_____

2) _____ said/or made me feel I am:

    (a)_____

    (b)_____

3) _____ said/or made me feel I am:

    (a)_____

    (b)_____

4) _____ said/or made me feel I am:

    (a)_____

    (b)_____

5) _____ said/or made me feel I am:

    (a)_____

    (b)_____

Continue on separate sheet of paper, if necessary.

Once your team's Press Interviews is complete, it's time to play and get your SCORE.

> **My Team Saw Me Naked**
>
> When I completed my Press Interviews, I was slightly surprised by some of my own results. There were a number of things I had forgotten. First, as an adult, many of my teammates view me as smart, wise, or bright, but when I was younger, many didn't. As I got older, many teammates viewed me as attractive but not so much when I was younger. Some teammates say I am a good leader, and a few consider me bossy.

Play the Game

Finished your Personal Bio? Finished your Press Interviews sheet? At this point, you could feel a little uneasy about your team, or you could feel ready for the playoffs. In this game, it doesn't really matter.

Now, from your Press Interviews sheet, copy your team members' names and comments onto your Game SCORE Card, according to the instructions below. It's okay to list your team members' comments in more than one section. Two Game SCORE cards are provided—one for you and one for your partner, if you are a couple.

1. It's likely that at least a few your team members have similar experiences when they're on the court with you. Get your Press Interviews sheet and look at your team's comments. Have some team members said the *same* thing or something similar about you? If yes, write the names of these team members and their comments in section S of your Game SCORE Card.

2. Who are your *coaches?* Coaches are those whose support or instruction impacts your game. They don't just give you

advice—they give you advice that impacts your game. If they are a skilled coach, they help you improve your game. If they are an unskilled coach, they may throw your game off. You can have more than one coach. Write down the name(s) of your coach(es) and their comments in section C of your Game SCORE Card.

3. It is possible that some of your team members experience you differently. You may play one way with a team member and switch it up when you play with another. Did any of your team members make comments about you that appear as opposites? If yes, write the names of these team members and their opposing comments in section O of your Game SCORE Card.

4. Players often develop a reputation. It's usually characterized by how we regularly perform during a game. Do you notice that some of the comments your team members have made about you regularly show up in your games? If yes, write the names of these team members and their comments in section R of your Game SCORE Card.

5. Your team name and Personal Bio reflect how you see yourself as a player. *Examine* your comments from your Personal Bio, then compare them to your team's comments, listed on your Press Interviews. Do any of your comments from your Personal Bio match up with any of your team's comments on your Press Interviews? Is the spirit of your team name reflected in any of your team's comments from your Press Interviews? If either of these are yes, write the names of team member(s) and their comments in section E of your Game SCORE Card.

Naked Basketball SCORE Card

	Team Member(s)	Comments About You as a Team Player	STRIP
S			
C			
O			
R			
E			

Continue on separate sheet of paper, if necessary

Naked Basketball SCORE Card

	Team Member(s)	Comments About You as a Team Player	STRIP
S			
C			
O			
R			
E			

Continue on separate sheet of paper, if necessary

What is your S-C-O-R-E?

S comments may suggest a characteristic or behavior that you likely exhibit whether you know it or not. If these comments are also in section E, you probably already know. If not, you may not be aware.

C comments represent your coaches' comments. These are important because coach comments impact how you play your game. Here, you may find comments that resonate with you or ones that conflict with your beliefs or values. If these comments are also in section E, it is likely you resonate with what is said. If not, there may be a disconnect between what your coach thinks is important and what you think is important.

O comments are potentially areas where you struggle. If these comments are also in section E, you probably already know this. If not, you may not be aware.

R comments are likely characteristics or behaviors you are aware of. If these comments are also in section E, you may embrace these characteristics and behaviors, or maybe they are areas you are currently working on. If not, perhaps you're not so proud of these characteristics or behaviors, and you'd rather ignore them.

E comments are characteristics or behaviors that you likely have examined or explored already. The fact that your team member(s) also see them suggests that you accept or embrace these traits.

Consider the Press Interviews comments or Bio comments that did not make it to your Game SCORE Card:

- Teammate comments that did not make it to your Game SCORE Card may suggest a different dynamic exists between you and that teammate. This may be something to consider as you continue to play these games.

- Coach comments that did not show up on your Personal Bio may suggest a coach who sees things in you that you don't see in yourself (your potential and areas for improvement) or one whose values or beliefs differ from yours.

- No Coach. What if you didn't list a coach? Not having a coach is rare. Even star players have a coach. So, not listing one may mean that you're not aware of who or what is influencing you. If no one person is your coach, then look beyond that. Do societal attitudes or events impact your game? Do certain public figures or celebrities impact your game? If you believe in a Higher Power, does that Higher Power impact your game? Or is there someone you'd never consider a coach, but whose scars and baggage impact your game? While not all coaches have the same skill level, any one of these could be your coach because of their impact.

- What if you disagree with a comment that your teammate has made about you? Since we are primarily focused on comments that more than one person has said, or that we ourselves have recognized, be open to exploring such comments. There may be an opportunity for you to expand your understanding of yourself.

- Your Bio comments that did not make it to your Game SCORE Card may suggest that either fear, stress, or worries are impacting your skills, as well as an opportunity to reassess your skills.

- No comments from your Press Interviews reflect the spirit of your team name? If this is the case, you may be playing a very different game than what you think you're playing.

Post-Game Wrap-Up: Let's Strip!

Some would argue the analysis that takes place during the post-game wrap-up is just as important as the score. Stats regarding shot averages, assists, rebounds, as well as evaluating moves, mental state, strengths, and limitations, help analyze performance and prepare for future games. So, Naked Basketball wouldn't be complete without doing a post-game wrap-up. Although, this version is more like a Post-Game Unwrap.

You're going to focus on your team members' comments from your Game SCORE Card and ask yourself a few child-like questions. Be honest and go as deep as you can. And don't avoid less desirable comments. In fact, less desirable comments can be more useful than desirable ones because criticisms and flaws can help us uncover pseudo-truths that are interfering and distorting our CORE truths. I've learned not to avoid looking at my faults because I know there is an opportunity for me to learn and grow. I find that which I struggle with most often exposes my CORE pseudo-truths, and eventually, the CORE truths that can energize me, instead of the fears that drain me. Our flaws simply reveal where we need to get naked by addressing our worries, insecurities, fears, and so on, so our relationship energy is not sabotaged by our CORE pseudo-truths.

Tips

- Determining a CORE truth: Let's say your spouse and mom say you are *helpful*. What's underneath? Does helping create a more stable home environment? Do you feel stable when you help? Then perhaps what's really important to you is stability. If so, *stable* is your CORE truth.

- Determining a CORE pseudo-truth: What if your friend and brother say you're *angry?* What fear or worry is underneath your anger? Are there certain aspirations or goals you've worked hard to achieve but haven't achieved, and you've become fearful of never achieving them? If so, then maybe you have a *fear of failure* and this is your CORE pseudo-truth. If you know this, you can work on it. If you don't, it can result in a habit of self-sabotaging behavior with no clear understanding of why. Also, once we work through the fear or pseudo-truth, our CORE truth can emerge. In this case, it's likely related to the goal or aspirations—not the fear.

Time to S-T-R-I-P!

S: SCORE Card. Get your SCORE Card. For each of the comments on your SCORE Card, answer these questions:

T: Truth or pseudo-truth? Remember, CORE truths and CORE pseudo-truths are what's underneath. When what's underneath are our fears, worries, stresses, insecurities, and so on, which distort our CORE truth, it is a CORE pseudo-truth. If it is based on a CORE pseudo-truth, skip the next two. Otherwise, go to the next question.

R: Results. Results are the basic reason we do what we do. So, let's get to what are the results of the characteristic or behavior used to describe you. Connect with your childlike curiosity and ask, "What happens because I do this or feel this way?"

I: Format your answer starting with:

"I_____"

Now write this CORE truth in the STRIP column.

P: Pseudo-truth: What is my fear, worry, insecurity, or stress? Write this CORE pseudo-truth in the STRIP column, then write "P" next to it.

- Instant Messengers: What instant messengers are influencing you? How does their influence match up with your CORE truths or CORE pseudo-truths? Are you aware of their impact on you? Instant Messengers, such as social norms or social class, are relentless instant messengers. How a society views you, good or bad, is a major influencer. For some, such instant messengers are their coach. Depending on the messaging, this kind of coach can improve or destroy your game. (If it's the latter, it's definitely time to find a new coach.) It's important to understand this as you play your game.

Foul Play

What if someone describes you as *stupid*, or you feel stupid? That definitely sucks. But the word *stupid* is meaningless. We may have been called stupid about something we do not care about anyway, but it was important to someone else—likely a coach. Or maybe we were called stupid about something we do care about, but we have been unable to master it. In either case, it's time to explore. It's likely this shows up somewhere in your CORE pseudo-truths.

Hey, Coach!

I discovered an unskilled coach who likely contributed to some of my struggles when I was younger: my mom. She passed away more than twenty years ago. I loved her dearly, and I know she loved me, but she was an unskilled coach. I identified her as an unskilled coach because her input tended to make me second guess myself and disrupted my game. I also realized fundamental differences between her values and my values.

For example, my mom valued the opinions of those who were affluent. If their children took piano lessons, then her daughter needed to take piano lessons. If their children dressed a particular way, then her daughter needed to dress that way. If their children went to a particular school, then her daughter needed to go to that school. Don't get me wrong—as a parent, I completely understand and appreciate wanting the best for your child. However, I've always had my own ideas and questioned just about everything.

Unfortunately, my inquisitiveness and independent nature were not applauded by my mother. She found them annoying and disrespectful. I recall this first becoming an issue for us from the time I was about eight years old continuing into my adulthood. While we ultimately came to an understanding and loved each other through it all, I realized that our ongoing challenges could have been reduced greatly had we focused less on who was right or wrong and more on recognizing and respecting each other's values and beliefs—and understanding each other's fears and stresses.

I also discovered another coach: an old friend. He was a skilled coach. When I was about fifteen years old, he encouraged me and believed in me. His input shifted my game and improved my game performance.

> In adulthood, I have had coaches who made me feel unstoppable. Currently, my two All-Star coaches are my spiritual teachers, Dr. Michael Bernard Beckwith of Agape Spiritual Center and Dr. Terry Cole-Whittaker, well-known speaker, teacher, and author.

Winning

Once you've analyzed your SCORE Card and STRIP—you're naked and you win!

When you STRIP down to your CORE truths, you better understand what you are bringing to your games. You also better understand the energy your teammates and coaches experience when you're running down the court, sitting on the bench, or just fouled out. You gain clarity and insight into you and your team—particularly when you and your partner are playing. When you both STRIP, you and your partner have the opportunity to understand and respect each other's CORE truths and strengthen your game.

Do fears, insecurities, worries, or stresses show up when you STRIP? That's good and that's normal. I don't know anyone who doesn't have CORE pseudo-truths: truths distorted by fears, anxieties, and insecurities that Create Our Relationship Energy. Acknowledging our CORE pseudo-truths and the fears, insecurities, and worries they are based on is very different from CORE pseudo-truths pretending to be CORE truths. When CORE pseudo-truths are acknowledged, they can be worked on. CORE pseudo-truths pretending to be CORE truths ultimately result in pseudo-connections.

In Chapter Three, we will focus more on uncovering our pseudo-truths.

But what if fears and stresses of a more serious nature—violence, substance abuse, chronic depression, health issues—show up? These can be extremely difficult to uncover and hard to face. If these issues show up, it is likely that they have shown up before. But just as an injured player needs special attention, we may need to seek special attention for such special circumstances. I strongly recommend that you seek consultation with a professional or support agency. If you are a couple, I suggest you both seek additional support.

END GAME

What About Your Partner?

This is a good time to bring your partner into your game. Share your team names and why you picked them. Have a little fun! Share your Personal Bio and Press Release with your partner. No doubt, they'll have a few comments of their own. And of course, share your SCORE card—particularly, your CORE truths and CORE pseudo-truths in the STRIP column. Your partner may learn a thing or two about you and vice versa.

Your Partner as Your Coach

As we've discussed, coaches can have a major impact on our game. Any star player knows the significance of a good coach. Frequently, the harder the coach is, the better the player becomes. Not only are you and your partner on each other's team, sometimes you and your partner are each other's coach. Like a good coach, you both are there to support each other as well as challenge each other.

For example, your partner may have an irritating habit of leaving messes around the house—clothes on the floor, dishes in the sink, or papers everywhere. Through their words and actions, your partner is about to coach you on how to skillfully navigate irritating situations. So, listen up. You may have an irritating habit of being late; you arrive everywhere at least fifteen minutes late. Through your words and actions, you're now about to coach your partner on how to navigate irritating situations. Remember, some of the best coaches are the toughest coaches.

But sometimes, nobody is the coach. Sometimes, you're just two players having fun and slapping each other on the butt!

By now, you should be naked. Therefore, it's time for another game! Our next game, *Double Dare,* is about experiencing a connection with your partner in which you both feel your core values and core beliefs are appreciated and supported. If you are ready for your right relationship, your next game is *Don't I Know You* (Level 1). This game is about exploring your connections with others. Interested in improving your connection with someone other than a spouse or significant other? Both of these games can be played with anyone you want to improve your connection with.

Ready for more naked play?

GAME

Double Dare

Rated: MC and S²
Game Rules

Object

This game is about creating relationship energy where your and your partner's CORE truths are supported. Want to improve your connection with someone close to you that's not your spouse or significant other? Pick a partner and let's play!

Set Up

It's necessary to play *Naked Basketball!* before playing this game. The purpose of *Naked Basketball!* was for you and your partner to STRIP down to your CORE truths and CORE pseudo-truths. Both are identified in your STRIP column. CORE pseudo-truths have a "P" next to them; CORE truths do not.

Getting Started

Once both of you have completed *Naked Basketball,* write down one or two of your CORE truths on a small piece of paper. For now, avoid any pseudo-truths related to fears or stresses—these will be used in another game. If only fears or stresses showed up for one or both of you, skip this game for now, and go to the next. Come back to this game when *both of you* have discovered at least one CORE truth.

- Take time to reflect on these and determine one or two ways they can be supported or encouraged by your partner.
- Now, swap papers with your partner.

Play the Game

- Designate a time period—one day, a weekend, one week, whatever feels right to both of you—to play this game.

- You will use the cheat sheet given to you and look for every opportunity to support your partner's CORE truths. For example, let's say *I like being reliable* is a CORE truth for your partner. You will do your best to respect that by doing what's on your partner's paper. Perhaps you've been asked to be more agreeable when your partner makes plans or be on time yourself. Do it. Remember, it's only for a designated time. And, your partner is doing the same for your CORE truths.

- Now it's time to experience what it feels like to trust someone and allow them to nurture your CORE truths. Both of you should totally forget about what you wrote on your own paper. Let it go and focus your complete attention on what your partner has written.

Winning
Share with each other what you liked most about the game and what you learned. If you and your partner both feel more supported, you've won the game.

Consider playing this game often. It is a good way for you and your partner to become more aware of each other's CORE truths and energize your relationship.

Challenge
Perhaps you or your partner are thinking: *This all sounds nice, but we have no time to do this stuff.* Well, you're kinda already playing. Whatever decisions you're making are based on CORE truths or pseudo-truths—truths that Create Our Relationship Energy. Ask yourself: *What kind of relationship energy are we creating? Do we have a habit of prioritizing everything else over our relationship? Is this the kind*

of relationship energy we want to create? If so, you might want to check how strong your connection is.

Weak connections result in frustrated communication that often leads to voids. How would you fill such a void, and where will you find the time? Our society, families, employers, and others put many time demands on us, so finding time may be the first challenge to overcome. But don't underestimate your resourcefulness and creativity. Besides, you or you and your partner set the time frame; the time can be as short or long as you choose.

END GAME

GAME

TRIPLE DARE

Rated: MC and S²
Game Rules

Object

Most of us are very aware of our partner's flaws—they're so easy to spot. And in some cases, there are so many of them, you just can't miss them. But this game is not about pointing out flaws. Instead, it's about understanding that fears, stresses, worries, insecurities, and anxieties distort or pretend to be CORE truths—and show up as CORE pseudo-truths. Want to improve your connection with someone close to you that's not your spouse or significant other? Grab the same partner you had in Double Dare and let's play!

Set Up

It's necessary to play *Naked Basketball!* before playing this game. The purpose of *Naked Basketball!* was for you and your partner to STRIP down so you can see and separate your CORE truths from your CORE pseudo-truths. While stripping, you likely discovered some fears, worries, stresses, and so on, distorting or pretending to be your CORE truths. These pseudo-truths are identified in your STRIP column with a "P" next to them.

If you are still struggling to identify your flaws, simply ask your partner. Then ask yourself: *What is the fear, insecurity, or stress that's contributing to it?* We're focusing on those distorted or hidden CORE truths that show up as your flaws. But, again, the idea is not to berate your flaws, but instead to dig deeper to uncover and understand the fears or stresses getting in the way of your CORE truths. Now, let's play!

Getting Started

Write down one or two of your pseudo-truths on a small piece of paper—any fears, stresses, worries, anxiety, or insecurities from your STRIP column (with a "P" next to it), or based on the flaws identified by your partner.

- Take time to reflect on these and determine one or two ways your partner could help you address these fears, insecurities, and worries.

- Now, swap papers with your partner.

Play the Game

- First, you should notice something different. Your partner's annoying habit or irritating behavior is stripped down, naked, exposed, and vulnerable. While you thought your partner was being difficult, now you see what's underneath that annoying habit and vice versa.

- Now, designate a time period—one day, a weekend, a week, whatever feels right to both of you—to play this game.

- During this time, each of you will do what is written on your paper to help your partner address their fears, anxieties, or worries.

- It's time to experience what it feels like to trust and allow someone to help you let go of your fears—if only a little bit. Both of you should totally forget about what you wrote on your own paper and focus your complete attention on what your partner has written on theirs.

Winning

If you and your partner feel a little more understood, you win the game!

END GAME

GAME

Don't I Know You?
(Level 1)

Rated: S²
Game Rules

Object

This game is about exploring your connections.

Set Up

You have to be naked to play this game, so if you did not play *Naked Basketball!* go back and STRIP before playing this game. In *Naked Basketball!*, we separate our CORE truths from CORE pseudo-truths. Get your SCORE card and look at your CORE pseudo-truths in the STRIP column. Remember, CORE pseudo-truths are based on fears, insecurities, and worries that Create Our Relationship Energy. Next, pick a group of people you know, either well or a little, for example, family members, friends, coworkers, classmates, group members; then figure out a time and place you will connect with them.

Getting Started

Next time you see them, do what you normally do, but mix it up just a bit. Observe them. How do they interact with others? How do they interact with you? Do they interact with others? Do they interact with you?

Play the Game

Do you notice anyone with your CORE pseudo-truths? Let's say your CORE pseudo-truth is *I'm afraid to make mistakes*. Do you notice anyone else like this? Let's say your pseudo-truth is *I don't want anyone* to take advantage of me (which could translate into, *I'm afraid someone will take advantage of me.*) Or, *I don't trust others* (which could translate into, *I'm afraid to trust others*). Do you notice anyone else who may feel like this? Let's say your CORE pseudo-truth is *I don't want to look stupid* (which likely translates into, *I'm afraid of looking stupid*). Do you notice anyone else who may feel this way too? It's possible to observe pseudo-truths through body language, facial expressions, and whether a person interacts with others. Obviously, it's better to have a little conversation with the person to get a better idea.

Tip

Pseudo-truths show up in different ways. Two people can have the same pseudo-truth, though it may show up differently. So, while you may laugh when you make a mistake, someone else may abruptly walk away, or make a joke, or be defensive. Just a little something to consider while playing. But, don't worry about whether you're right or not. This is a game—It's not about being right.

Winning

If you found at least one person with your CORE pseudo-truth, you win! (Even if you're wrong.) You get bonus points if you found more than one person.

Challenge

What if you don't have any CORE pseudo-truths? Okay. If you say so. Then skip this game and go to Level 2. However, I don't know anyone who doesn't have CORE pseudo-truths. When we acknowledge our CORE pseudo-truths, we can work on them. CORE pseudo-truths pretending to be CORE truths ultimately result in pseudo-connections. What if you find it hard to determine other people's pseudo-truths? You're thinking too much. Just observe people and do your best.

END GAME

Chapter Two

I've Met My Match: My Perfect Match

When we venture into a relationship, we are often looking for that perfect match. Even those whose goal is not marriage may still want that perfect person who won't bug them when they are busy and who is ready to have fun when they are free.

When we meet our perfect match, we are so excited. They like movies, just like we do. They like sports, just like we do. They like hiking, just like we do. OMG—the perfect match! During this stage of a relationship, we are excited, energized, and little bothers us. Our relationship is fun and easy—at least for the moment—usually the first three to six months.

Now, I do believe it is possible to find our perfect match. However, that person won't be perfect, right? Then why do we struggle with those pesky imperfections when they show up? Why are we so surprised when we discover our partner has major flaws? The problem may lie in what we define as *the perfect match*.

We often think the perfect match means there will be few arguments, if any, and we will get along well. We usually have a list of qualities that we desire: smart, funny, good-looking, financially stable, or passionate. Additionally, we think they'll *get us* and understand our moods, feelings, and actions with little effort on our part. Some of these qualities may exist in a relationship, and probably should exist to some extent. However, it is unlikely all these qualities will exist and exist all the time. In fact, if they all do exist all the time, I would wonder if someone is suppressing their CORE truths, or if they even know what their CORE truths are.

The perfect match probably sounds appealing because so many things in our lives challenge us. We are challenged by work, challenged by finances, challenged by family members, challenged by school, and challenged by life. How good it is to find someone who is a respite from all those challenges. Instead of *the perfect match,* we perhaps need a phrase that better describes what some of us are really seeking.

Here are a few possibilities:

- Vacation Match
- Hobby Match
- Make Me Look Good Match
- Make Me Feel Good Match
- Make Me Forget All My Problems Match
- Don't Cause Me Any Problems Match
- Let's Do What I Want to Do Match
- Just Do What I Say Match
- Take Care of Me Match
- Make Me Happy Match

What do you think?

Which of the above are you, or which do you want to be?

While the idea of having one of these perfect matches for yourself may be quite appealing, ask yourself if you are as enthusiastic about being one of them. Do you find having a "Make Me Happy" match to be equally as satisfying as being the one charged with making the other happy? And what happens in the Make Me Happy match when what makes one person happy doesn't work for the other? However, there are people who may not mind being the compliant one in the Make Me Happy match.

If this is you, I have just a few questions:

- How do you handle fulfilling someone else's needs while having yours ignored?
- What are your CORE truths, and how does this type of relationship support them?
- Are there CORE pseudo-truths, fears, or stresses that you're currently dealing with?

When reviewing your answers, seriously consider if you are interested in being in a power^{ed} relationship or simply interested in being in a relationship. Also, consider you may have given up on yourself. If either of these are true for you, I encourage you to continue reading and playing. Whether you realize it or not, you always have the final choice.

The problem with the above perfect matches is that they create a one-directional relationship. We become fixated on what we want and whether we are receiving it. When we add the rest of life to that fixation, there is little time to understand what the other person needs, let alone to fulfill those needs.

What happens when one or both people in a relationship are focused on getting what they want? Well, you could either end up with a barter system relationship that feels rather hollow and cold or a relationship with one or two disappointed people.

Life is not one directional. If we want to connect to the power of life, we cannot be one directional. Nature teaches us if we plant seeds in fertile soil and we properly water and care for those seeds, they will grow and give us food. The richer the soil and the more attentive we are, the more abundant the harvest will be.

However, if the soil is depleted, we need to work much harder to make our seeds grow. We may become exhausted in the process and may not have much of a harvest, if any. If the soil is rich, but we fail to provide water and care, we'll have rich soil and no harvest. Of course, it is useless for us to buy seeds and carry them around in our pocket. Once we have the right seeds in the right soil, we must water and care for them. Otherwise, they will not properly grow for us—no matter how much we complain.

Regardless of how much attention we give our perfect match, things will not always go smoothly. In a relationship, there is the lovemaking and then there is the labor. Lovemaking can be blissful and exciting, but labor is often painful and quite messy. Even with the most perfect match, there's labor involved. But labor can birth new qualities in you and your partner. Challenges can grow you, your partner, and your relationship. Together, you both can decide how to address various issues so that you both feel your CORE truths are supported. If you both decide outside advice is necessary, that's fine, but don't give up your power as a couple, and definitely don't zone out.

As discussed in Chapter One, with so many messengers vying for our attention and living in a society that bombards us with constant change, we may lose sight of our CORE truths. This impacts not only us, but our relationship or how we approach starting a relationship.

We want to ensure our match choices and relationship energy are based on our own CORE truths rather than someone else's ideas, opinions, propaganda, or marketing strategies.

The next two games, *Perfect Strangers* (Level 1) and *Naked Tic-Tac-Toe*, are about exploring your relationship energy and choices. *Perfect Strangers* (Level 1) is for couples who are married or in a committed relationship to reconnect with their perfect match. *Naked Tic-Tac-Toe* is for singles to see how their CORE truths match up with their match choices.

GAME

Perfect Strangers (Level 1)

Rated: MC
Game Rules

Object

After being with our partner for a while, we can begin to feel disconnected. Busy lifestyles and time demands can drain your relationship energy and leave you and your partner feeling like strangers. When this happens, it's the perfect time to reconnect. If you and your partner are feeling a like strangers, you're going to act like strangers—*Perfect Strangers*.

Set Up

You and your partner are going on a date. But before you meet, you must each decide who is showing up.

You have three choices:

- Your current self
- Your previous self (when you first met your partner)
- Your fantasy self

You and your partner do not have to pick the same *self*. Your partner can be their current self and you can be your fantasy self. However, neither of you will know whom you are meeting with until your date.

You each will prepare for this date as you would for any first date. So, if you would dress up for a first date, then dress up. If you would wash your car for a first date, then wash your car. If you would get your hair cut or your nails done, then get your hair cut or your nails done. If you would pack a small overnight bag in case you got lucky, then pack your overnight bag (no judgment from me). If you would normally meet at a particular location, then consider taking separate cars. Remember, this is your first date. Don't blow it.

Play the Game
As with any first date, you will politely introduce yourselves. Even if you both show up as your current selves, still treat this like a first date in which you are meeting each other for the first time. Even if you know everything about your partner and they know everything about you, forget everything you both know—or think you know—and be in the present moment. Forget about everything and stay connected. Enjoy this perfect stranger. Have fun!

Winning
Winning is easy. If you both had fun, you both win.

END GAME

GAME

Naked Tic-Tac-Toe

Rated: S
Game Rules

Object

Does your idea of your perfect connection matchup with your CORE truths? This game is about comparing what you say you want in your perfect match to your CORE truths.

Play the Game

First, list up to four traits that describe what you want in your perfect match:

_____

_____

_____

_____

Now, let's look at what influences how you choose your perfect match. Is it family and friends? Is it media and celebrity icons? Is it your CORE truths, or is it your CORE pseudo-truths?

Below is a diagram for your *Naked Tic-Tac-Toe* game. Simply fill it in according to these instructions:

1. **Your CORE Truths:** In Chapter One's game, *Naked Basketball!*, you stripped down to your CORE truths and pseudo-truths. Refer to your SCORE card and the CORE truths in the STRIP column. List three CORE truths on each line in the first column under YOUR CORE TRUTHS.

2. **Media and Celebrity:** Is there a movie, TV show, magazine, or celebrity that captures your perfect match? On each line in the second column under MEDIA AND CELEBRITY, list those traits perfectly reflected by that movie, TV show, magazine, or famous person.

3. **Family and Friends:** Family and friends often have ideas regarding who is the perfect match for us and what traits we should look for. On each line in the third column under FAMILY AND FRIENDS, list the traits your friends and family feel make the perfect match for you.

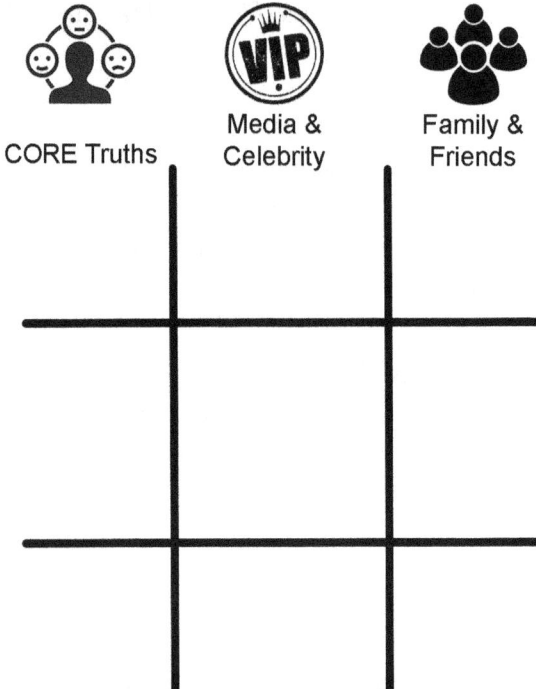

1. Look at the four traits on your perfect match list.
2. For each of the traits from your list, look at your *Tic-Tac-Toe* game and find matching traits. Draw an **O** around all matches.
3. Do this for each of the four traits you listed as traits you desire in your perfect match.
4. Once you have matched all four of your desired traits, mark an **X** on the traits that do not have **O**s.
5. Find which group has the most **O**s: your CORE truths, media and celebrity, or friends and family.
6. Draw a tic-tac-toe line through the column that has the most **O**s.

The winner: _____

Winning

CORE Truths Wins

If this category is the winner, congratulations on basing your perfect match your CORE truths. Also, congrats on not basing your perfect match on your CORE pseudo-truths, which reflect your fears, insecurities, and stresses.

Media and Celebrity Wins

If this category is the winner, congratulations on paying attention to what type of traits or person you desire. Remember that the most appealing traits presented in the media and celebrities are often amplified. They are designed to appeal to us. Check to ensure your perfect match's traits are not just appealing to the masses but compatible with your CORE truths.

Family and Friends Wins

If this is the winner, congratulations on paying attention to family and friends who know you and, no doubt, want the best for you. However, check in to ensure these perfect traits align with your CORE truths.

Challenge

What if you don't like what's influencing your match choices or noticed your CORE pseudo-truths are actually influencing your match choices? You may feel uneasy, but don't worry. In subsequent chapters, you will have opportunities to explore what may be creating a disconnect in your search.

Bonus Challenge

So, what about the Xs? Look at the traits that have an X. Are these traits important to you? If so, don't forget about them. These X traits may simply be traits you are less conscious of, but if they are important, consider becoming more conscious of them. If they are not important to you, then perhaps they are simply important to someone else and therefore not applicable to your perfect match.

Finally, what if one of your desired traits did not show up in your *Naked Tic-Tac-Toe* game anywhere? Don't overthink it. If it is important, it's important. If it's not, it's not. Just be clear if it is or it isn't. However, if it's related to a CORE pseudo-truth, there's more play to do.

END GAME

Have you ever pursued a relationship, career, or education, and when you finally had it, thought to yourself: *Is this all there is?* If so, it's likely you had a disconnection between your CORE truths and your decision process. Ultimately, we have power over who and what we choose to accept into our life. Power[ed] people use that power.

Chapter Three

Dance Class: Remember Your Backpack

The first part of this chapter may seem more applicable to those ready for their right partner. However, if you are married or in a committed relationship and are following the sequence of this book, you recently had a date with your perfect match. You also have another one coming up—so read the entire chapter.

First dates are such unpredictable encounters. Don't you agree? First dates remind me of starting a new dance class. If you've ever taken a dance class, you know they can be really fun or really frustrating. While a new dance class is exciting, and we may be eager to learn some new steps, we still can experience a little anxiety. Will we embarrass ourselves or glide across the floor? Hopefully our feet will cooperate, but we won't know for sure until we start dancing.

Do you recall your last first date? Maybe it started off like many. You thought to yourself: *This one's cute*. You found yourself eager to see if there was a connection. Maybe the initial conversation started with something like: *What is your name? What do you do? What do you like to do?* Yada, yada, yada. These are typical conversation starters. Maybe you found the person interesting and they liked you too. Perhaps things continued fairly well until they said something that bothered you. Hmmm. Perhaps they hold a viewpoint that doesn't quite fit with yours. You thought to yourself: *Oh, that's okay. Everyone is different; everyone has their own opinion.*

Fast-forward a couple dates and a few months later, when someone asks how things are going, and you reluctantly reply:

- *Well, it didn't work out.*
- *They were too busy.*
- *Are you kidding?*
- *I have no idea what happened.*
- *I'm seeing someone else now.*
- *Who?*
- *I'm taking a break.*

Repeat these moves enough times and this dance could leave you out of breath. But, perhaps, there is another approach. Let's repeat.

Here we go again. You meet someone and think to yourself: *This one's cute.* You find yourself eager to see if there is a connection. The initial conversation starts with something like: *What is your name? What do you do? What do you like to do?* Yada, yada, yada. These are typical conversation starters. You find your date interesting and they are interested in you too. Things continue fairly well. Then, they say something that bothers you. Perhaps they have a viewpoint that doesn't quite fit yours.

"Hmmm," you say, "I'm curious what you mean by that?"

You listen to their response, and then you check in with your gut. How does your gut feel about this?

Many of us are familiar with gut instincts, but few of us probably follow them. Our gut is a good internal gauge and often just as quick to respond as other parts of our body. Even if we are unaware, we usually have a gut reaction. We often cause ourselves problems when we ignore our gut instincts and focus on more precarious parts of our body to guide us. It is not uncommon for our mind to even talk us out of listening to our gut instincts.

Core Work

When we dance, our abdominal area—our core—is our source for balance and stability. However, our core does more than help our dance moves look graceful. This internal gauge should be given respectable attention—perhaps even more attention than we give to its external form. The abdominal area has long been associated with hunches; hence the expressions *gut reaction or gut instincts*.

In sacred Eastern teachings, the abdomen is referred to as the *third chakra*. And while chakra studies involve our seven primary energy centers, or chakras, this third chakra is considered the body's energy center where our personal power resides.

Another reference indicating the importance of our abdominal area is found in traditional Christian teaching. Many Bible buffs are familiar with the reference, "Fasten the belt of truth around your waist." (Ephesians 6:14, BSB) Yes, our gut is worth paying attention to. So, how might a gut-check impact our dating response?

While our head might say: *Everyone is different and has their own opinion,* our gut may say: *This person isn't a good fit for me.* Fast-forward a few months later when someone asks how things are going and you may reply, "They were okay but just not a good fit for me."

First, just because someone is not a good fit for us does not mean they are not a good person. We don't have to cross someone off like a wrong answer. If that person isn't a good relationship match for us, we do not need to deride them, make excuses, or lose hope. We also don't have to accept someone into our life if we have a hunch that they are not right for us.

Have you ever given someone the benefit of the doubt and been sorry you did? We don't always need to give someone the benefit of the doubt if we sense they are not a good fit for us. If we gave everyone we felt was not a good match the benefit of the doubt, we might never connect with the person who is a good match. At the same time, we don't want to pick someone apart, looking for perfection.

So, where is the happy medium?

Pack Your Backpack

The word *baggage* is often used to describe our life experiences, perceptions, and ideas regarding personal relationships that have challenged us. Our baggage is often a combination of our family dynamics, past relationship challenges, prejudices, and fears. However, to effectively access our gut instincts, we need to leave our baggage at home.

However, a small backpack is useful. Your backpack should include the essentials: your CORE truths and those qualities that support and enhance them. Include receptive listening and sincerity, and that's it! You're ready to go.

There is no room for fears, worries, or insecurities in your backpack. And, if you are tempted to take your suitcase with you, I suggest emptying out everything onto your bed before you leave. That way, if you do carry it with you, it will be empty. When we clear out our baggage, it is more likely our hunches are true instead of triggers from our past or present fears, prejudgments, insecurities, or unrealistic ideals. To effectively access our gut instincts, it's about tuning into our instincts as much as it is about turning off our fears and insecurities.

Now, let's repeat this encounter one more time.

You've packed your CORE truths, your qualities that support and encourage them, and your receptive listening and sincerity. Every day, you place these in your backpack before you gather up your other stuff and head out the door You leave your suitcase of CORE pseudo-truths at home—you'll deal with these another time.

One day, you meet someone and you think to yourself: *This one's cute.* You find yourself eager to see if there is a connection. The initial conversation starts with something like: *What is your name? What do you do? What do you like to do?* Yada, yada, yada. These are typical conversation starters. You find your date interesting and they are interested in you too. Things continue fairly well. Then, they say something that resonates with you. Perhaps they love hiking, and let's say, *love of nature* is in your backpack.

"Please tell me more about that," you reply. You eagerly listen to their response and when you check in with your gut, it says: *I like it!* This listening is different from the example before because instead of listening for what you don't like, you are listening for what you do like at the core level. Let's say you love hiking because you value nature and love being outside. A partner who values nature is important to you.

Fast-forward a few months later when someone asks how things are going and maybe you reply, "We are still dating. We both love being outdoors, and we are planning a camping trip for this weekend. We don't agree on everything, but we are having a lot of fun."

If having a power[ed] relationship is our goal, we need someone who fits our CORE truths, and we need to fit theirs. If we know our CORE truths, we can better determine this. Lugging around a suitcase filled with fears, worries, insecurities, and past relationship challenges leaves little room for our CORE truths—not to mention the misery of carrying around such a heavy load. We must swap our baggage for a small backpack. If we don't, we are left to choose based on superficial qualities: *How does the person look? What do they do? How much money do they make? Do they go to the gym?* Or worse, we choose based on our fears, worries, insecurities, and past relationship challenges. There is nothing wrong with assessing a person's looks, career, or financial status, but these qualities are unlikely to contribute to your CORE truths or a power^{ed} connection.

So, after a first few encounters that look promising, then what?

Let's Dance

Recognize that the party is just getting started, and it's a dance party! Sometimes the dance is salsa; sometimes it is tango, hip-hop, waltz, or line dancing. It won't always be the same beat, look the same, or feel the same. So, you need to pay attention. If you desire a power^{ed} relationship with someone who complements your CORE truths and vice versa, then it's important you both move to similar rhythms. When two people both know their CORE truths, they can share them with each other, and the fun can truly begin.

This experience becomes a playful adventure—one in which you talk, share, and do things you both enjoy while still allowing time to do those things you enjoy as individuals. Don't diminish the experience by taking things too seriously or worrying: *Where is the relationship going? When will we have sex? Will we stay together? Will it lead to marriage?* Instead, focus on the dance and on learning the CORE truth of the other person while staying aware of your own.

Waltz or Line Dance?

A common misconception is that when we become a couple, our time must be reserved for each other. Yes, we want to spend time with our partner, but we do not need to consider everyone else an intruder. Instead of looking at people and external situations as impositions, it's best to *open the dance floor and learn some new steps.* You need to get to know the people and activities the other person is involved in, and they need to learn the same about you. As appropriate, and when opportunities arise, get to know the person's friends and family.

The people and activities in our lives contribute to who we are and help others know us. Furthermore, it is important to understand that life is always happening, so we need to remain creative and flexible. But what do we do if we have been with our significant other for a while and need some new moves?

Ouch! You Stepped on My Foot

Maybe you and your significant other have been together for a while, but now one, or both or you, feel something is missing. Everything was great when you first got together, but something has changed—your dance moves aren't as smooth as they use to be. After we have been with someone for a significant period, we begin to discover things about them that we may not have paid much attention to in the beginning. Frequently, these are things we don't particularly like.

For example, maybe we didn't realize how bossy or messy our partner is. Maybe we didn't realize how differently we view finances or family activities. No doubt, they are discovering similar things about us. From my observations, couples who have remained connected over a long period of time have successfully overcome such obstacles. They don't deny their partner's faults or their own. It's not so much they overlook their partner's faults as they understand them.

At times, you may feel more like being a spectator than getting on the dance floor. Of course, every day cannot be a tango. If it were, you both would be exhausted and little else would get done. However, your CORE truths should always be dancing. If you are already a couple and you want to improve your connection and move past some of the missteps, the next games may help your moves.

Often, couples make the mistake of comparing their relationship to others: *Oh, if we only had a relationship like Demetri and Karla! Oh, if only my wife looked like Sophia! If only my husband made the money that James makes!* Our relationships are not limited to others' ideals, social norms, or celebrity images. We do not want to base our relationships on fantasies, social trends, or anyone else's relationship. You and your partner are the only ones who have power over your relationship. Together, you both get to decide what's important and what is not when working to stay connected. The music will not be the same every day; the dance will not always be the same. It won't necessarily look like another couple's dance, either. Who leads and who follows will change as the music changes. In one situation, you will take the lead, and in another, your partner will take the lead. It is entirely up to each couple to determine what mix works best for them. And when your toes get stepped on, retrace your own steps and help your partner do the same. It may be time to change the tempo or even the dance—but keep on dancing. Who should lead? Who should follow? It totally depends on your dance.

Practice, Practice, Practice

It's game time! We have two new games. The next game for couples is *Perfect Strangers* (Level 2.) It is the next level of *Perfect Strangers* (Level 1) from Chapter Two. The next game for singles is *Don't I Know You?* (Level 2) and is the next level of Chapter One's game. Both games are about connecting based on CORE truths—the truths that Create

Our Relationship Energy. In both of these games, you're taking your backpack and leaving all other baggage at home.

GAME

Perfect Strangers (Level 2)

Rated: MC
Game Rules

Object

Perfect Strangers (Level 2) is the next level of Chapter Two's *Perfect Strangers* (Level 1). All the rules are the same except one—make sure you bring your backpack on this date. And make sure you emptied out your suitcase and left all CORE pseudo-truths at home, absolutely all of them.

Set Up

You and your partner will schedule a date. But before you meet, you must each decide who is showing up.

You have three choices:

- Your current self
- Your previous self (when you first met your partner)
- Your fantasy self

You and your partner do not have to pick the same self. Your partner can be their current self and you can be your fantasy self. However, neither of you will know who you are meeting with until your date.

You each will prepare for this date as you would for any first date. So, if you would dress up for a first date, then dress up. If you would wash your car for a first date, then wash your car. If you would get your hair cut or your nails done, then get your hair cut or your nails done. If you would pack a small overnight bag in case you got lucky, then pack your overnight bag (no judgment from me). If you would normally meet at a particular location, then consider taking separate cars. Remember, this is your first date. Don't blow it.

Important: Don't forget to bring your backpack. On this date, your backpack is essential.

Play the Game

As with any first date, politely introduce yourselves. Even if you both show up as your current selves, still treat this like a first date when you are meeting each other for the first time. Even if you know everything about your partner and they know everything about you, forget everything you both know (or think you know) and be in the present moment. Forget about everything and stay in the present moment. Enjoy this perfect stranger. Have fun!

Winning

Winning is easy. If you both had fun, you both win.

Bonus Win

You and your partner had more fun on this date than your first date.

END GAME

GAME

Don't I Know You?
(Level 2)

Rated: S²
Game Rules

Object

This game is about exploring your connections—at a higher level.

Set Up

You've played *Don't I Know You* (Level 1). Now it's time to take it to a new level—Level 2. As in Level 1, you have to be naked to play this game. Again, in *Naked Basketball!*, we separated our CORE truths from CORE pseudo-truths, so get your SCORE card and pick out a CORE truth from the STRIP column. Now, plan to meet up with the same people you did in Level 1. If you did not play Level 1 because you have no CORE pseudo-truths, pick a group of people you either know well or are a little familiar with, for example, family members, friends, coworkers, classmates, group members, and figure out a time and place you will connect with them.

Getting Started

When you meet up with your people, again, do what you normally do, but mix it up by observing their interactions. How do they interact with others? How do they interact with you? Do they interact with others? Do they interact with you?

Play the Game

Do you notice anyone with your CORE truths? Let's say your CORE truth is *I am stable*. Do you notice anyone else who is? Let's say your

CORE truth is *I am creative*. Do you notice anyone else who is? Let's say your CORE truth is *I like being around people*. Notice anyone else like this? Yes, it's possible to observe CORE truths through body language, facial expressions, and how a person interacts with others, but it's better to have a little conversation with them.

Tips

Like CORE pseudo-truths, CORE truths can show up in different ways. The person who is stable may be more helpful or more reserved. The person who is creative may be interested in trying out new things or have an outside-the-box view of things. The person who enjoys being around people may be friendly or a jokester. Again, don't worry about whether you're right or not. This is a game—It's not about being right.

Winning

If you found at least one person with your CORE truth, you win! (Even if you're wrong.) You get bonus points if you found more than one person.

Challenge

What if you find it hard to play this game? What if you don't have any CORE truths? Hmm. I don't know anyone who doesn't have any CORE truths. If this is your experience, maybe your coach encouraged you to operate from fear, or you don't have a coach, or you are unaware of who your coach is. Don't worry. Remember, fears, worries, and insecurities interfere and distort CORE truths. We all have CORE truths. You may need to work harder at addressing the CORE pseudo-truths to get to your CORE truths. Keep playing all the games in this book. After you complete this book and all the games, go back and play *Naked Basketball!* again.

END GAME

Chapter Four

The Feminine Fuse: Inspire Higher

In all relationships, there is play between the masculine and feminine energies, and power^ed relationships have similar rules of play. In power^ed relationships, masculine energy is often purposeful and driven, interested in expansion, and committed to something beyond self. There is also a compelling feminine energy that is more than nurturing. It is a delicate balance of force and tenderness that parallels the force and tenderness that births and sustains life. From this feminine energy, the growth and expansion of each person within the relationship, as well as the relationship itself, is ignited. I call it the *feminine fuse.*

Men and women have both masculine and feminine energies, so in no way is this to suggest that females cannot be purposefully driven and committed or that males cannot be tender. My point is to simply acknowledge and explore the power of feminine inspiration within the power^ed relationships and the impact it has on potent masculine energy. When we consider our favorite power^ed couples, could the magic we admire in their relationship reflect this power^ed feminine inspiration, the fuse?

Masculine and feminine energies are at play in all relationships, so it is important to consider this play particularly in our own relationship. Feminine energy is organic; it is perceptive, nurturing, and alluring. Power^ed feminine energy can ignite potent masculine energy, causing it to expand and explode. Masculine energy is territorial, competitive, and commanding. Power^ed masculine energy can provide safety and stability, allowing feminine energy to release and flow.

The question is: Are the masculine and feminine energies at play in our relationship powering our relationship or draining it?

Inspired to Inspire

Let's say you are a woman who wants to inspire her man, but you're not sure how. Releasing your power^ed feminine energy can be an effective way to do so. However, I am not referring to something that is contrived or calculated. Nor should this energy do for the masculine what he can do himself, as doing so may undermine power^ed masculine energy. Inspiring our masculine partner rarely comes from carefully developed strategies or clever conversations, and it is unlikely that we will *figure out* how to be his inspiration.

True inspiration is intangible and cannot be faked. Being his inspiration is as much about being who you fully are as it is about inspiring him to be who he fully is. But this exchange is not a competition. This is about bringing the best of who you are and inspiring the best in your partner. Your inspired words and actions are much more profound than reciting carefully scripted phrases.

To be inspiring, you must feel inspired. If you don't feel inspired, it is difficult to inspire someone else. To feel inspired, you may need to take time for yourself to determine what inspires you outside of your partner. Those outside things that deeply move you can become a catalyst, not only to you personally, but also to your relationship.

Therefore, explore what moves you, what makes you flow. This exploration should be more than receiving pampering massages, reading romance novels, or decorating your body with artful tattoos—although these can be meaningful too. Seek inspiration by being actively involved in what feeds your CORE truths. Become an intense force, grounded in power[ed] love, inspired, and equipped to inspire.

Being in a state of inspiration requires commitment, clarity, and action. It requires paying attention to how we are feeling and not allowing ourselves to get caught up in routine activities. We must nurture ourselves first before we can nurture our significant other or anyone else for that matter. But again, this is not about pampering ourselves, although being pampered is important. This is about nurturing our CORE truths.

The key difference between pampering versus inspiration is this: When we are in a pampered state, our energy and focus move *from outside* ourselves to inside ourselves; we are in a state of receiving. This includes giving to ourselves, which I also consider pampering—and important. When we are in an inspired state, our energy and focus move *from inside* ourselves to outside of ourselves; we are in a state of giving to others. Furthermore, there is nothing we are trying to gain for ourselves because we are fulfilled. We give from a place of abundance, not a place of lack. As we are inspired, we will inspire others, including our significant other.

Next, you should know what you value in your partner, what you believe about your partner, and what their CORE truths are. From a place of inspiration, not provocation, you support and encourage your masculine's CORE truths and what you value in him. It is from this place that masculine energy can be ignited.

However, if we don't really feel it, we can't really inspire it. We may be tempted to inspire our partner to be something we hope or want him to be, even if we are not sure he is capable of our expectation. That could be considered manipulating, but it is definitely not inspiring.

It is also possible we may not be genuinely moved to inspire anything in our partner. If this is the case for you, this could be a good time to explore your partner's CORE truths and your own—and your pseudo-truths as well. Refer back to your SCORE card and review your STRIP column and, if possible, sit with your partner and review your SCORE cards together. Are there any CORE truths or CORE pseudo-truths getting in the way? Are there any conflicts? If so, how about a game of Double Dare or Triple Dare? If that's not an option, then have a discussion about what showed up AFTER reading the next chapter—*Timeout: Good and Bad Arguments*. If you both don't feel comfortable talking about all your CORE truths and CORE pseudo-truths with each other, then discuss why you don't feel comfortable AFTER reading the next chapter.

What if the masculine desires his feminine partner to be more inspiring and, maybe, less demanding?

Masculine Devotion

Power^{ed} feminine energy flourishes when it feels safe and at ease. Stress or fear can make power^{ed} feminine energy retreat. When the feminine feels threatened, she is likely to revert to weaker feminine energy and seek refuge in the masculine. Therefore, a woman who does not feel supported by her partner may appear irrational or seek refuge in a masculine surrogate—or in her own masculine energy. If you want to encourage power^{ed} feminine inspiration in your partner, try providing stabilizing masculine energy.

In this instance, connecting with your power^{ed} masculine energy is not about having irresistible swagger. Though, who is to say you won't? It's about understanding your woman's CORE truths and needs, then doing what you can to support them. And it's about action—not just talk. Of course, your ability to fulfill her need will depend on the need.

For example, if she needs help because she is overwhelmed by the demands of work and home life, have a heart-centered talk and listen for what you can do. Then, just do it. However, if she is having issues with her family, you are probably limited in what you can do as she must learn and grow from her own experiences. You can still listen for what you can do to support her in her growth process. Then, just do it.

As the masculine, you are prone to bottom lines and getting things done. When a woman is in her masculine energy, she may respond in a similar manner. But if you want your woman to gravitate toward her power[ed] feminine energy, she will need your heart-centered devotion so she can release this energy.

Now let me be clear, this is not about doing everything for your woman, yet it involves more than being a spectator in her life. This is about bringing what you love and value about her to your conversations and listening from a place of devotion so you can support her CORE truths. Like inspiration, devotion cannot be faked. If you cannot honestly demonstrate this level of devotion, or if you still feel uninspired, this could be a good time to explore your significant other's CORE truths and yours.

But what if caring for your feminine partner makes you feel subservient or less masculine? I have seen all types of devoted pet owners feed, provide water, then pick up poop after their beloved pet—but by no means am I suggesting going this far. Again, there's a difference between being helpful and supportive and being responsible for cleaning up someone's mess. But caring for someone we love should bring some level of satisfaction. If it doesn't, then maybe look at your CORE pseudo-truths. Is your relationship energy with your feminine partner based on fear, stress, insecurity, or worry?

Refer back to your SCORE card and review your STRIP column and, if possible, sit with your partner and review your SCORE cards together. Are there any CORE truths or CORE pseudo-truths getting in the way? Are there any conflicts? If so, how about a game of Double Dare or Triple Dare? If that's not an option, then have a discussion about what showed up AFTER reading the next chapter—*Timeout: Good and Bad Arguments*. If you both don't feel comfortable talking about all your CORE truths and CORE pseudo-truths with each other, then discuss why you don't feel comfortable AFTER reading the next chapter. Yes, you can sit quietly while she rants, thinking about what you're going to do once she stops talking. But it is likely she will either retreat to weaker feminine energy and become more emotional or gravitate toward her own masculinity in order to stabilize herself, becoming more aggressive in the relationship and, of course, less inspiring to you.

Now, it's game on! Time to learn a few things about inspiration from two of our favorite creatures. To assist us with becoming more inspiring and supportive to our significant other, we're turning to two of our most beloved inspirations.

GAME

LOVE YOUR PET

Rated: MC
Game Rules

Object
To inspire your affection connection—and have fun!

Getting Started
We love our pets. We are so inspired by them. So, who better to learn from? To help us get started, here is a little background information on two of our most beloved pets.

Pet #1
We love Pet #1 because they are so adorable. They are curious creatures who love their freedom; they just love to roam. They love sniffing the ground and discovering new territory. They love to play and can find countless ways to amuse themselves. Most love to have their heads or necks rubbed, but most of all, they love to have their bellies rubbed. Most are fun-loving and like to jump on you and lick you when you come home. You must give these pets clear instructions—it's either *yes* or *no*. They ignore *maybe* and inconsistent messages confuse them. If you say, "No, don't dig holes in the back yard," and you sit back while

they dig holes in the back yard, you will end up with a backyard full of holes. If you are not sure what you want them to do, they will certainly not know what you want them to do and will do whatever they want. But, when you take time to understand Pet #1 and they trust you, they will love and protect you and do what they can to make you happy.

Pet #2

Pet #2 is also cute but a little different from Pet #1. Pet #2 likes to play too—but when they want to. They prefer a nice, clean litter box and their food and water in a convenient location that they can easily get to. Pet #2 may spend a little more time grooming themselves than Pet #1. They can spend hours and hours making sure their fur is soft. They like to observe things. Usually, they will thoroughly check you out before they let you touch them. They like to cuddle, and they do like to have their fur stroked, but it must be the right way—not too hard, the right direction, and not too fast. One more thing: these pets are likely to scratch you if you rub them the wrong way. Some feel that Pet #2 is too finicky. But when they feel safe and loved, they will rub against you and lie in your lap.

Play the Game

Pet #1 Lovers

Set aside time—a few hours or a day—it's your choice. During this time, lavish your love and attention on your *pet*. When your pet walks in the room, kiss and rub your pet's head or neck, even if you are tired. Talk sweetly to your pet and make your pet feel your love. If your pet needs to go outside or to another room to play, give your pet the freedom to roam. And if you catch your pet digging where you don't want or destroying one of your favorite items, clearly set your boundaries, but continue giving your love. Play with, cuddle, and enjoy your pet and remember to give plenty of belly rubs when the time is right.

Pet #2 Lovers

Focus your attention on providing for your pet for a set time period—several hours or a day—it's your choice. Before even being asked, provide what they need. If you're not sure what those needs are, ask in advance so you can have everything ready beforehand. If your pet isn't clearly communicating what they need, postpone this game for a few days. Observe and access what you think their needs are. Once you have an idea, do your best to provide them. Check in with your pet and be available in case something else comes up. And if your pet decides to rub against you or lie on your lap, cuddle with your pet and go with the flow.

Winning

You and your partner win when either of you is rubbing, licking, or lying on the other's lap.

END GAME

GAME

Your Perfect Pet

Rated: S

Game Rules

Object
To inspire our affection connection—and have fun!

Getting Started
We love our pets! We are so inspired by them. So, who better to teach us how to express our affection? To help us get started, here is a little background information on two of our most beloved pets.

Pet #1
We love Pet #1 because they are so adorable. They are curious creatures who love their freedom; they just love to roam. They love sniffing the ground and discovering new territory. They love to play and can find countless ways to amuse themselves. Most love to have their heads or necks rubbed, but most of all, they love to have their bellies rubbed. Most are fun-loving and like to jump on you and lick you. You must give these pets clear instructions— it's either yes or no. Maybe confuses them. If you say, "No, don't dig holes in the back yard," and you sit back while they dig holes in the back yard, you will end up with a backyard full of holes. If you are not sure what you want them

to do, they will certainly not know what you want them to do and will do whatever they want. But, when you take time to understand Pet #1 and they trust you, they will love and protect you and do what they can to make you happy.

Pet #2
Pet #2 is also cute but a little different from Pet #1. Pet #2 likes to play too—but when they want to. They prefer a nice, clean litter box and their food and water in a convenient location that they can easily get to. They typically put more time into grooming themselves than Pet #1. They can spend hours and hours making sure their fur is soft. They like to observe things. Usually, they will thoroughly check you out before they let you touch them. They like to cuddle, and they do like to have their fur stroked, but it must be the right way—not too hard, the right direction, and not too fast. One more thing—these pets are likely to scratch you if you rub them the wrong way. Some feel that Pet #2 is too finicky. But when they feel safe and loved, they will rub against you and lay in your lap.

Play the Game
A responsible pet owner fully considers their situation before they get a pet and will only get a pet once they feel they can properly care for it. Are you sure you're ready?

If you prefer Pet #1, remember they are often fun-loving and may want to jump on you, lick you, and go home with you. Some are so cute that you may be tempted to bring them home, but don't get sidetracked—you want to find the right pet for you. Also, keep in mind, all breeds are not the same and may need to be approached differently. Some breeds may be more guarded and must be approached cautiously. They may need to feel comfortable with you before they let you touch them. So, consider checking out different breeds before you decide. Visit places that have the breeds you like. This allows you to play with a few and see how you bond before making a final decision.

If Pet #2 is your choice, you may find them hanging out in groups. This could be a little overwhelming for you, as you might think to yourself *they all have such pretty fur,* but stay focused! They can be quite social, although sometimes they just want to be left alone. Because Pet #2 can be finicky, you want to pick the right one for you. Remember, you might be preparing their litter box or providing fresh food and water for them. When approaching them, it doesn't hurt to be a little cautious. Take your time—talk to them, get to know a little about them. They like it when you make them feel comfortable.

Winning
If you felt inspired in your search for a pet—you win!

Challenges
What if you felt uncomfortable or frustrated in your search for a pet? What if you just don't feel inspired? Maybe you're not yet ready to pick your pet. Maybe you need to do a little more exploring. Or maybe you've got your baggage with you. Go back to Chapter Three and play *Don't I Know You* (Level 2), so you can clean out your backpack a little more before you go exploring again.

END GAME

Chapter Five

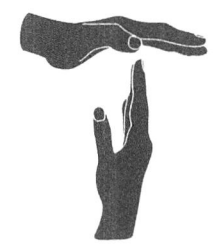

Time-Out: Good and Bad Arguments

Relationships can be tough, sometimes really tough. We can be confronted with issues that seriously challenge us and our communication with our partner. Maybe a sensitive issue upsets us and perhaps upsets our partner too. Maybe past discussions have ended in arguments and nothing was resolved. Pretending everything is fine, ignoring issues, or sucking it up does not resolve an issue or nurture a relationship; passivity is not a remedy for dealing with sensitive issues. There will be difficult issues that require attention and discussion. These issues provide the relationship and both individuals an opportunity to evolve. When these occur, we need to take a *time-out* to discuss tough issues.

Before any words come out of our mouth, it is best to first check our thoughts and feelings. We should not deny our feelings as they should be given proper respect. When disagreements with our partners arise, we may feel exasperated, particularly if we feel strongly about our perspective. Remember, our partner is not our enemy. We desire a conversation with someone who we care about, not a fight to the finish. The last thing we want to do is engage in a power struggle with the person we love.

So, when sensitive issues arise, how do two people who love each other exert their power without engaging in a destructive power struggle?

In my own experiences, I have observed there are two key elements that impact a challenging issue. If it is a tough issue, either the person I am talking to or the issue is important to me. If it is an extremely tough issue, it is usually both. This is likely true for most of us. We need to recognize this and take it to heart because it reminds us to give proper care, respect, and attention to a matter without getting caught up in egoistic power struggles and victimhood or passively blowing it off.

When divisive behaviors hack into our communication, they take our attention from what is important, and nothing is resolved. Entering a tough discussion by giving our issue and our partner the proper love and respect will not guarantee we will get what we want, but it will allow for the best possible outcome. It allows each person to be heard at the heart level. It is at this heart level that our communication is power^{ed}.

No matter how hard we try, though, our attempts to have a calm, cool conversation are unsuccessful at times. If you and your partner argue—and it is likely you will, at least a few times—have a *good* argument. A good argument is far better than keeping your hurt, anger, pain, and confusion inside, letting it fester until the discussion turns into a bad argument.

A Good Argument

I must admit that I prefer a good argument over meaningless chatter. Some of my best communication has occurred in an argument. In these arguments, I was expressive, passionate, and honest and so was the other person. Not only was my conviction clear, it was clear how important the topic was to me and for the other person. I put all my feelings on the table, as did the other person. Usually, both of us struggled to be understood. Some of my arguments have ended with resolution and some have not.

Why do some arguments end with resolution while others do not? I have noticed there are subtle differences that make arguments productive or make them fail. Good and bad arguments have similar characteristics: emotionally charged, strong viewpoints, the need to be understood, and loud. You can probably think of a few others.

In retrospect, my *bad arguments* contained specific elements that made the arguments fail:

- At least one person tried to control the discussion.
- At least one person needed to be right.
- At least one person was condescending, belittling, or self-righteous.

My *good arguments* contained elements that made resolution possible:

- After a few rude interruptions, one person finally stopped and listened.
- After saying or hearing the same thing over and over again, one person finally felt what was being expressed—sometimes through tears.
- Both people remained committed to the relationship.

Nothing can be accomplished through a bad argument. Often, no one is paying attention to the point of a bad argument, including the people talking.

What is the point of a bad argument? Let's see. You got something off your chest? Okay. You felt superior? Okay. You made the other person feel bad or look stupid? Okay. But you also probably damaged the relationship, and nothing was really resolved. But again, that does not mean you should remain silent about your concerns.

Twelve Rules for a Good Argument:

1. Do not try to control each other.

2. Do not belittle each other.

3. Do not keep score.

4. Do not play mind games or use sarcasm.

5. Do speak your feelings passionately, completely, and honestly.

6. Do all you can to make the other person understand why this topic is important to you.

7. Do cry if you need to.

8. If someone must hit something or throw something *absolutely do not* direct it at each other. Make sure the object is something that won't break—pillows, bean bags, sandbags—something you can fix, or you both can live without.

9. If you must yell or scream, try to keep it low enough so the neighbors don't hear you.

10. If you were committed to the relationship before the argument, stay committed through the argument.

11. If discussing sensitive topics, keep focused on respecting your feelings and each other.

12. Speak from and listen with your heart.

Some issues can be resolved with the first argument, but sometimes they are not. What is significant is that you and your partner feel better understood. It may take several discussions or good arguments before a resolution becomes clear, but in the process, you can still build your connection to each other rather than destroy it. I've also found it best to resolve issues within a forty-eight-hour period, if possible. The likelihood of resentment is greatly reduced, particularly built-up resentment, which is probably the most destructive. Additionally, I'm prone to mulling things over and looking at the situation from different perspectives before I approach a difficult conversation. Including this in the forty-eight-hour time frame allows me to avoid overthinking it—*analysis paralysis*.

If we're feeling bombarded or overwhelmed, finding the time to resolve issues can be challenging. We need to be creative. Face-to-face conversations are preferable, but not always possible. If necessary, reserve face-to-face discussion for critical issues. Otherwise, you can write notes to each other, leave voice messages, or text—however you can effectively communicate with minimal delay.

Through this alternative correspondence, you can either set up uninterrupted time for a discussion later or, if appropriate, begin the discussion. You need to make sure you and your partner agree on the method of communication before issues arise. I've also learned that some things can be resolved without a long discussion with my husband. At times, my own growth is what is necessary.

Being a couple does not mean that I, as an individual, stop growing. Solutions can be found through talking to the other person, but they can also be found by talking to the person in the mirror.

How can we determine which situation requires a discussion with our partner and which one does not? As a rule of thumb, I ask myself: *What can I do or change to make this situation better?* If my actions would be reasonable and they resolve the issue, then there probably is no reason to discuss it with my husband. If my actions alone do not resolve the issue, my husband and I need to have a discussion.

But what if outside influences are impacting communication with our partner?

Static Issues

Have you ever failed to reach a resolution after opening lines of communication to your partner? Even after having a good argument? If no matter how hard you and your partner try, you simply cannot resolve the issue, maybe there are outside influences getting in the way of your communication. Perhaps *static* is impacting your communication. Static disrupts our communication, and when it is present, it's almost impossible to have a real discussion. One person says one thing, and the other person hears something completely different and vice versa. The best way to resume clear communication is to remove the static. When static is removed, it is possible to have clear communication that leads to a resolution. But before we can remove static, we need to know what it is and where it is coming from.

Static can show up in our communication in many ways, but its presence may not be obvious. Static can be hard to detect. It can show up as previous relationship fears, financial concerns, trust issues, or just about anything. Because static can be hard to detect, it may require a concerted effort to find it.

Below, I have listed common static issues that can disrupt communication. Consider those issues you and your partner have been unable to resolve. Could any of these static issues be inhibiting your communication? Can you or your partner think of a few others? Whatever static you discover, consider having a discussion or good argument regarding these static issues before you tackle your main issue. This step allows you to remove the static so it does not interfere with your primary conversation, as well as gives you both an opportunity to address or resolve underlying concerns.

Possible static issues:

1. Money problems
2. Sex or intimacy concerns
3. Family issues
4. Trust concerns
5. Health problems
6. Tired or lack of sleep
7. Problems at work

I Don't Want to Play Anymore

What if you're questioning whether you should even remain in your relationship? This is a tough, if not impossible, question for someone to answer for you. Of course, that does not mean you won't get plenty of advice. Only you can answer this question. Again, this book is about powering you, not you giving your power to someone else.

It's probably time to take a close look at the game you and your significant other are playing. You and your partner may currently feel disconnected. Are your CORE truths connecting? Are you both willing and able to support each other's CORE truths? Have you had several good arguments? Can you both up your game by clearing out your suitcases?

Do you have children? A couple with children is playing a much more complex game than a couple who recently started their relationship or don't have children. But whether you have children or not, if your partner plays a significant role in your life, it's likely they'll always be on your team in some way or another, even if they are just sitting on the bench. For example, your *ex* may continue to be with you through *your* resentment, fears, anger, lessons learned, or personal growth. I simply suggest considering all this in your decision process.

If you are experiencing extreme issues such as domestic violence, any form of abuse, or health issues, these are serious problems beyond the scope of this book. In these cases, I strongly suggest seeking professional and legal advice.

Time to play! For couples, *Can You Hear Me Now?* is a fun way to observe how static can impact your communication. *Do I Know You?* is about getting past the barriers that disrupt our communication. This is a good game for both singles and couples.

GAME

Can You Hear Me Now?

Rated: MC
Game Rules

Object
To identify broken connections between you and your partner.

Set Up
Who is the better communicator in your relationship? Who is the better listener? Who is the clearer thinker, and who is all over the place? Discuss plans for your next date. In your discussions, who is likely to stay focused and who is easily distracted? Is one of you a better communicator while one of you struggles to stay on point? Does one of you talk too much or not talk enough?

Getting Started
Grab two pieces of paper and two pens. Then go sit in separate rooms—where there are distractions. One of you go into a room and turn on your favorite TV show or one you enjoy. The other one, go into a room where you can turn on music—loud music—or somewhere kids are playing, neighbors are loud, and so on. The idea is to be somewhere distracting. You have up to four minutes to play this game.

Play the Game
With the distractions around you, take your paper and pen and do the following:

- List cars that start with the letter A.
- List cars that start with the letter B.

- List cars that start with the letter C.
- And so on . . .
- After two minutes, you both will stop and count how many cars are listed on your sheet.

Winning

You and your partner will compare your lists. The person who listed more cars, wins.

Challenge

You and your partner will need to move past any confusion, anger, or pain to play this game.

Go to the next page after you determine who won.

Bonus Win

Did you notice that winning this game had nothing to do with planning your next date? The Game Rules said you were to discuss plans for your next date. Did anyone bring this up? Did you and your partner complete plans for your next date?

The winner of this game was the person who had more cars listed on their paper. Of course, this doesn't make sense. What does listing cars have to do with planning your next date? Nothing.

Take a moment to answer the following questions:

- Have you ever been so caught up in your own thoughts or activities that you failed to give adequate attention to the topic you're discussing with your partner?

- Have you ever started a conversation with your partner about one thing and ended up arguing about something else?

- Have you ever won an argument where you set the other person straight, but the primary issue was left unresolved?

These scenarios don't make sense either. Even if we win an argument, it does not mean our relationship wins. If you and your partner completed plans for your next date, you both win.

Still unable to find the rule about discussing your next date? Go back to Set Up and look for the following: Who is the better communicator in your relationship? Who is the better listener? Who is the clearer thinker, and who is all over the place? *Discuss plans for your next date.*

Now, who would you say is the superior communicator? If neither of you brought up plans about your next date, I would say it is a draw. While one of you may have listed more cars than the other, the objective to plan your next date was never discussed. Does the person with the better arguments, the quicker wit, or the more creative zingers really win an argument if the primary objective of the conversation is lost?

If one or both of you did discuss plans for your next date and didn't get sidetracked by counting cars—congratulations! Your ability to stay on task and not be sidetracked by outside distractions has been validated!

Actual Objectives of This Game
You and your partner feel how static can distort your communication.

END GAME

GAME

Do I Know You?

Rated: MC and S²
Game Rules

Object
This game is about troubleshooting connections.

Set Up
Is there someone you struggle to get along with? Do you struggle in conversation or to be in the same room? Is there a group of people with whom you struggle? Of course, I'm not talking about anyone who has threatened you or wants to cause you harm. But do you struggle simply to understand this group of people? You're looking for a person or people you just don't connect with or, when you do connect, your wires cross. For example, is there a coworker you avoid or a family member you struggle with? Or is there a particular group of people you feel uncomfortable around? If you're a couple, could communication between you and your partner use a recharge? Couples, you play this game with your partner. Everyone else, pick a person or a group and let's play!

Getting Started
Once you decide whom to play with, you need to decide where to play. If it's a coworker, you can play at work. If it's a family member or your partner, you can play next time you talk to them. If it's a group, you'll need to find a spot where this group is. One more thing—you need to have your CORE truths and CORE pseudo-truths handy. This game is best played impromptu—and the other player(s) doesn't even need to know they're playing with you! The game starts when you say you're ready to play the game.

Play the Game

This game has three levels and you get to decide the level you play at. But it's good to play all three levels, especially if you are a couple. The levels are explained below.

When you're with the other player(s), you're going to observe them a little differently than you normally do. Rather than the usual disdain or agitation, you're going to decide how you want to play with them.

Level 1 – Think about your CORE pseudo-truths, then observe this player(s.) Does this player(s) have a similar CORE pseudo-truth? If you observe similar CORE pseudo-truth in the other player(s), remember what it is.

Level 2 – Think about your CORE truths then observe this player(s.) Does this player(s) have a similar CORE truth? If you observe a similar CORE truth in the other player(s), remember what it is.

Level 3 – Think about your CORE pseudo-truths and observe this player(s.) Does this player have CORE truths you can learn from? In other words, is there something you struggle with that this player does well? If you observe a CORE truth in the other player(s) that you can learn from, remember what it is.

Level 1 players, you and the other person share a CORE pseudo-truth. Do you also share a similar struggle or feeling? Allow yourself to feel this connection and remember it the next few times you see them.

Level 2 players, you and the other person share a CORE truth. Do you also share a similar passion or feeling? Allow yourself to appreciate this CORE truth in the other person and feel this connection. Remember it the next few times you see them.

Level 3 players, you may hate to admit it, but they've got something you want. Don't hate. Now, it may take a little more observation to determine if it's their CORE truth, manipulation, or opportunistic tendencies you're seeing—but look for their CORE truth. And when you conclude it's their CORE truth, if it's not counter to your CORE truth, consider trying their approach (or some version of it) next time you're struggling with your issue. Hey, if it works, remember that the next few times you see them.

Winning

Did you complete one or more of the three levels? You win!

Challenge

Yeah, this game is supposed to be challenging. Maybe you couldn't complete any of the levels? Remember, this is a game! Don't take it too seriously. You only need to complete one level to win—try again.

END GAME

Chapter Six

Show and Tell: Sex Conversations

Sex. This word has such magic and power. Mention the word *sex*, and eyebrows raise and ears flutter. Sex brings up various images, thoughts, and feelings for each person and means different things to different people in significant ways. However, have you ever noticed that sometimes when we talk about sex, we are really not talking about sex at all, but rather, things related to sex?

I think it's safe to say that in its most simplistic form, sex is pretty straightforward: arousal, climax, and procreation (maybe). Simple. However, sex is also associated with feelings of desirability, attraction, pleasure, power, control, submissiveness, love, connection, closeness, compassion, affection, self-expression, excitement, adventure, frustration, reinvigoration, pain, and even fear. Of course, these feelings can be experienced in nonsexual ways, too. But when they show up in sex—well, sex becomes a little more complex.

Other than childbirth, sex is the only physical act I can think of that can deeply connect two people. With the variety of attitudes and responses to sex and potentially intense physical connection to another person, it's not too hard to understand how we may end up with—well—complex sex.

Sex triggers emotions that reveal our deepest desires, as well as influences how we respond to each other. It is not my intention to take the romance, passion, or what we desire out of sex, and I know I risk sounding too clinical with this question, but have you ever considered that romance, passion, or whatever we desire are actually things we bring to sex, rather than what we get out of it?

Think about it: Aren't the attitudes we bring to sex reflective of what we feel we need to give or receive from sex? If this is true, then sex becomes a blank canvas on which we create our own sexual montage.

If we love someone, we may look to sex to express that love. If we are attracted to someone, we may look to sex to express that attraction. If we feel unloved, we may look to sex to feel love. If we feel disempowered, we may look to sex to feel empowered. If we are frustrated, we may look to sex to release our frustration. An interesting dynamic can emerge from this mixture of self-expression, need, and sex. Knowing and understanding the different ways we use sex in our intimate relationship can be the difference between confusion and satisfaction.

If my partner feels disempowered and chooses to use sex to feel empowered, while I feel unloved and choose to use sex to feel loved, our sexual encounter could be disappointing, to say the least. If my partner aggressively approaches sex while I am seeking tenderness, sex can leave one, if not both of us, feeling bewildered and unfulfilled. But the issue is not our sex. The issue is how we are both feeling and how we bring those feelings to our sexual connection. In these moments, it may be a good idea to have a *naked conversation*.

Naked Communication

In the earlier chapters, we talked about being naked. We talked about completely stripping—shedding our excuses, our judgments, and any egoistic facades—and uncovering our true selves. What if we brought this kind of nakedness to our sex conversations? What if we approached our sex conversations with the same openness, honesty, understanding, passion, and courage that we approach our other conversations?

Obviously, we would need to be rational, knowing that in the same way we cannot expect to get everything we want from our partner outside of sex, we cannot expect to get everything we want from our partner in sex. We would also want to avoid any shame or judgment regarding what we each want to bring to the sexual experience. This environment of freedom and acceptance allows our self-expressions and needs to be revealed and explored through our sexual experience. Also, as with any other aspect of our relationship, our CORE truths and our partner's CORE truths should be considered.

Often, sex conversations are not about sex at all. Sex is really simple: arousal, climax and procreation (sometimes). When we are in a naked sex conversation with our partner, it's probably best not to get too caught up in discussions about frequency, positions, or sex paraphernalia unless we really want to talk only about sex. If we want to talk about our self-expression and needs in our sexual experience, then it's best to stay focused on that and leave frequency, positions, or sex paraphernalia for another time.

Sometimes naked sex conversations can be more difficult than a typical sex conversation because they reveal more intimate details about us—our vulnerabilities, our expectations, our insecurities, and our complexities. Talking about frequency, positions, or sex paraphernalia is often much easier. If our partner doesn't like a suggestion, we can always blame someone else's bad idea: *It was a horrible book, movie, or magazine.* We don't risk our partner judging us, or even worse, rejecting us. But when we have naked sex conversations, we open the doorway to deeper trust and a deeper connection with our partner. Otherwise, sex is very simple.

But how do we go from simple sex conversations about frequency, positions, and sex paraphernalia—or perhaps no conversations about sex—to more complex conversations? How do we have naked sex conversations?

Show Your Self
Since we are talking about self-expression, needs, and desires, a naked sex conversation is not much different from any other conversation. The biggest difference is the inclusion of how these needs play out in our sexual relationship. For example, my partner may be feeling disempowered at a time he needs to feel powerful. In discussing his feelings of disempowerment, my partner and I may explore those feelings and ways I can help him feel empowered—in the bedroom and beyond the bedroom. If I am feeling unloved or unworthy, my partner and I may explore those feelings and ways he can make me feel loved—in the bedroom and beyond the bedroom. These conversations can add depth to our sexual experience as we seek to fulfill not only our partner's physical needs but their CORE desires as well and vice versa.

As in any other conversation, our expressions and needs may be different from our partner's. However, if we remain open, our differences can actually add a provocative dynamic to our sex conversations as well as our sexual connection. Naked sex conversations can power a relationship, as they allow for deepened physical and emotional self-expression, which can ignite both partners' desire to satisfy each other.

Again, a safe and accepting atmosphere is critical to naked sex conversations, because without it, sex conversations could result in repressed feelings, repressed behaviors, or even resentment. But with honest and open sex conversations, you and your partner create opportunities to deepen not only your sexual relationship, but your overall relationship. These conversations allow you and your partner to better understand what you each bring to sex and enable you both to fully express and better fulfill each other's deeper needs.

As you and your relationship evolve and you grow, your self-expressions and needs can change. This changes what you bring to your sexual experience. You should approach these shifts with the same attitude you approach any other changes in yourself or your partner.

What if you find sex conversations challenging?

Tell Me a Bedtime Story

Sex conversations can be challenging even in the most accepting relationship. For example, if someone with an active sexual history marries someone who is a virgin, they may find sex conversations a little uncomfortable, and it's likely they have different concepts about what should be brought to the sexual experience. Additionally, though there is a range of sexual attitudes within each gender, it is not uncommon to find differences in men and women regarding how often they think about sex and what they think about.

Regarding male sexual fantasies, a University of Washington study reported, "The most common men's sexual fantasies are about (their) partner doing things they wouldn't ordinarily do."[1] In comparison, a survey regarding female sexual fantasies makes the following suggestions to women, "So, if you find yourself going through the week without a sexual thought, make a conscious decision to change that!"[2]

Regardless of the situation, honest and open communication that respects the personal expression and personal needs of both partners is essential. It is imperative to avoid judgment and demonstrate

---

1 Vann, Madeline. *Top 10 Sexual Fantasies for Men*. Everyday Health. everydayhealth.com/mens-health-pictures/top-sexual-fantasies-for-men.aspx#01
2 Berman, Laura. *10 Favorite Female Sexual Fantasies*. Everyday Health.

flexibility so that both partners' CORE truths are supported and CORE pseudo-truths are not shamed.

Some couples may need to ease into sex conversations. Sharing our intimate feelings or most desirable sexual encounters with our partner may be a good way to start. Our next game, *Bedtime Stories,* provides creative ideas about how to start these conversations. However, whether you and your partner struggle with sex conversations or not, *Bedtime Stories* can be revealing and fun. After completing your first bedtime story, you and your partner may want to consider sharing your bedtime stories on a regular basis.

If you are single and looking for your perfect match, the game *Private Monologues* is for you. It is your playful exploration and expression of what stimulates your sexual core.

GAME

BEDTIME STORIES

Rated: MC

Game Rules

Object
To create a power surge in your sexual connection.

Set Up
If you or your partner feel you could use a little inspiration, allow individual time to enter a sensual state before you begin playing this game. Include whatever puts you in your most sensual state—candles, music, your favorite toy, your favorite outfit, your favorite magazine, your favorite book, or your favorite movie.

Getting Started
Option 1: Separately, you and your partner take time—a couple hours, a couple days, or a weekend, whatever you both decide—and write down your intimate feelings or sexual encounters that personally appeal

to you. Don't rush. Allow your imagination to roam and include as many details as possible.

If you prefer, use video or voice recording . . . just keep track of it.

Option 2: If you don't consider yourself the creative storywriting type, select one of your favorite sex stories, movies, books, pictures, or songs to share with your partner.

If you choose this option, reflect on what you like about it. Then write down, voice record, video record, dance, sing, draw, or be ready to express your sexual enthusiasm with your partner! This is not about summarizing your selection. This is about expressing how you feel. Share your selection with your partner and do what you can to make sure they know how much you like it.

Here are some examples to help you start:

- When I hear this story, it makes me feel_____.
- When I see this picture, it makes me think about_____.
- When I watch this movie, it makes my body_____.
- When I hear this song, it makes me want to_____.
- I particularly like the part about_____ because_____.

Body language is also strongly encouraged.

Tip: If you don't already have a favorite, go on an exploration until you find something you really like.

Play the Game

Share your *Bedtime Story* with your partner. Also share how your bedtime story makes you feel.

Tip: When it's time to share your bedtime story (voice or video recording, picture, magazine, movie, and so on) with your partner, it may be fun to prepare your space and yourself as you may have done for your own bedtime storytime.

Good bedtime stories do not have to be told in bed or when you're ready to go to sleep. They can be told any time of the day and anywhere: a restaurant, the park, the beach, or even in the car.

For an erotic adventure, you could arrange a time with your partner and act out your desires either at home or at a location you feel is more suitable.

If you are short on time, leave your story or selected story, picture, and so on, somewhere that your partner can easily find them—on their pillow or in the bathroom (assuming no one else uses this bathroom).

With so many options, each partner can take a turn in setting the atmosphere for sharing their story. It's up to you and your partner—just bare it all! Be as creative as you would like; just be careful that your stories don't fall into the wrong hands.

Winning
I'll let you and your partner decide this one.

Challenge
As tempting as it may be, I encourage you and your partner to reserve this time only for *storytelling*—which means no sex—at least for the first couple of times you do it. This will allow each partner to fully express their sexual desire without worrying about what's next. The other person simply watches, listens, and takes it all in.

This game is about each partner being intensely aware of what stimulates them and sharing that with their partner. This game is *not* about what you can do to turn your partner on. In this game, it is about *turning yourself on* while your partner watches and listens. Try saving sex for later. You will find it worth waiting for.

Note: If after sharing, either of you find this encounter too intense, consider finishing with *solo performances*. And yes, your partner can be your audience.

But what if you find it difficult to share your sexual feelings with your partner? Maybe you feel ashamed or afraid of being judged or laughed at. Or, maybe you just don't know where to begin. If this is the case, play *Private Monologues* before playing *Bedtime Stories*. It's a game for singles, but it can help you become more comfortable with your own sexuality. Once you win *Private Monologues*, try playing *Bedtime Stories* again.

END GAME

GAME

PRIVATE MONOLOGUES

Rated: S
Game Rules

Object
To stimulate your sexual power source.

Set Up
If you feel you could use a little inspiration, allow yourself time to enter a sensual state before you begin. Include whatever puts you in your most sensual state—candles, music, your favorite toy, your favorite outfit, your favorite magazine, your favorite book, or your favorite movie.

Play the Game
Option 1: Take time—a few hours, a few days, whatever feels comfortable to you—and write down intimate feelings or sexual encounters that personally appeal to you. Don't rush. Allow your imagination to roam and include as many details as possible.

If you prefer, use video or voice recording. Please, keep track of it.

Option 2: If you don't consider yourself the creative storywriting type, select one of your favorite sex stories, movies, books, pictures, or songs.

If you choose this option, reflect on what you like about your selection, then express how it makes you feel and why. You can write it down, voice record, video record, dance, sing, draw, or use whatever form of self-expression you want. This is not about summarizing what the selection is about. This is about expressing how you feel.

Tip: If you don't already have a favorite, go on an exploration until you find something you really like.

Tip: Occasionally exploring your own sexual desires helps you stay attuned to and comfortable with your own sexual feelings.

Staying attuned to your own sexual feelings is important for a couple reasons:

1. First, we often are bombarded with sexual messages in our day-to-day experiences. Without revisiting our own sexual desires, we may either succumb to someone else's sexual ideals or turn our desire completely off. In my opinion, neither is desirable.

2. When we do enter a relationship, we will be able to better express our sexual desires to our partner.

Winning
If you have enjoyed this game—you win!

Challenge
Not able to get in the mood of this game? Don't worry about it. Instead of focusing on sexual exploration, find time to relax. Relax your body, your mind, your emotions. Though this may sound too simple, simple is likely what you need. Lie down comfortably and just breathe. Breathe and feel your lungs and belly expand and contract. Listen to your breath and don't think about anything else. Start with

five minutes two times a day and work your way up to fifteen minutes two times a day. After about a week or two of relaxing, try your sexual exploration again.

END GAME

Chapter Seven

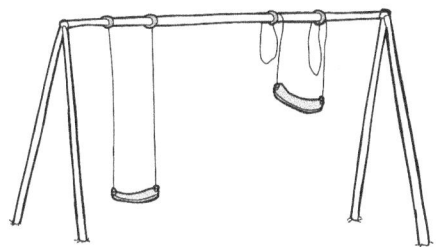

My Favorite Playmate: Laughter Is Romantic

Have you found your soul mate? Whether you have or not, let me ask you a better question: Have you found your *playmate?* Connecting on a soul level is important to nurturing our CORE truths. However, I would argue that finding our playmate is equally important.

Remember the excitement and fun you experienced when you began dating your partner or when you began your most memorable relationship? Remember how eager you were to be around them?

Without some level of fun, we are unlikely to pursue a relationship. And if we do, there are likely other dynamics related to CORE truths or pseudo-truths. But if fun played a part in developing our relationship with our partner, doesn't it make sense that fun would be important to sustaining it?

Romance is important to a relationship—no doubt—and we should allow time to make our partner feel special and vice versa. However, I sometimes wonder if we put too much emphasis on romance and not enough on enjoying each other by simply having fun.

We all have physical, mental, and spiritual abilities, and our emotions—how we feel—have a major impact on how these abilities perform. How we feel impacts whether we jump out of bed or crawl out of bed. How we feel impacts whether we ace a test or struggle. How we feel impacts whether we feel connected to a Higher Power or feel completely isolated. Our emotions impact how we function and how we function in our relationship. Can you see why taking time to play and have fun together is important for us individually and as a couple?

Ever watch children playing their favorite game? They are full of energy and joy. Some of the best friendships are formed on the elementary school playground. Playtime puts our emotional dial at its best setting. We are recharged, re-energized, and fun filled. And play time with our partner not only recharges us but also re-energizes our connection to our partner. When we emotionally connect at play, we connect with our partner at a deeper subconscious level, which is one of the reasons this book is devoted to play. Regularly playing with our partner allows our bond to deepen.

When two people are having fun, laughing uncontrollably, and gazing into each other's eyes, what happens? What emotional and physiological connections are made? It's anyone's guess, but it's got to be something good!

Our Playtime

In this complex world, making time for play can be challenging. The longer we are in a relationship, the more responsibilities we have and the harder it becomes to find the time to play with our partner. Additionally, people may frown upon play and associate it with frivolity, but we need playtime. Without sufficient playtime, we become cranky and burned out both as individuals and as couples. Depending on our schedules, we may have playtime once a week, once a month, once a quarter, or perhaps, even once a year. The more the better, of course. The activity can be anything.

Maybe it's playing or watching basketball, football, or baseball; watching movies or listening to music; playing board games, cards, or video games; singing or dancing; cooking; hiking; or biking. Whatever the play is, the point is to have fun. Even if it's only once a year, commitment to full-on playtime at least once a year—several days of vacation—is better than no playtime, and the anticipation of doing something you absolutely love with someone you love gives you and your partner something to look forward to.

And I wouldn't rush to schedule that vacation and then forget about it until it's time to pack your suitcase. As you plan, talk to each other, leave notes for each other about what you're personally looking forward to, or make suggestions of how to enjoy the vacation more. Planning your playtime should be part of your play. Don't underestimate the power of play.

It's a Laughing Matter

Real life provides the best comedy and this includes our relationships. Those who have been in a relationship for a while know that relationships can be fun, interesting, and downright entertaining—sometimes without even trying. Personally, I've always enjoyed humor and approached it with curiosity.

Everyone does not laugh at the same thing. One person may find something funny while another may find it completely offensive. Like anything else, our life experiences usually dictate the differences. This is something we should be sensitive to when playing with our partner. The longer we are with our partner, the better we understand what is funny to them and what is not.

Additionally, there are serious times when something happens, and we feel anxious, upset, or concerned. But after a while, that same situation suddenly becomes funny. Over time, we exhaust every possible way of seeing a troubling situation until it finally loses its edge. Then one day, we find ourselves sharing that experience with someone and laughing at it, wondering: *Wow, when did that become funny?*

What if we could fast-forward that sense of humor to a situation as it is happening, instead of waiting several years? Think of the pain we could save ourselves and the time we could gain to be more productive.

When I have a healthy sense of humor about a challenging situation, I'm not as defensive and neither is my partner. Most of the time, he laughs too. Again, I am not talking about making fun of someone (unless it is myself) or belittling the importance of the situation. But I have gotten to a point where I truly find some things I do quite funny. And since I recognize some of these quirky things about myself, I laugh if my husband brings them up—and trust me, he does.

My husband and I both have strong personalities. In our discussions, we each declare our opinion or judgment as if we are the voice of authority. We have both accused the other of being opinionated and a *know-it-all*. The reality is we probably both are. Now, without a sense of humor, this could become really ugly. When one of us makes a declaration and it proves to be wrong, you can bet that the other one takes notice. Neither of us likes to be wrong, but sometimes the one in error can't help but laugh. There have been times that my edicts have been so off base, I couldn't keep myself from laughing.

My husband also has a great sense of humor. In fact, he is downright funny. He also laughs at some of the idiosyncratic things he does. In this lighter state of mind, we are less combative, more open, and less argumentative. This is not to say that everything is a laughing matter, but sometimes couples make situations more serious than they need to be. In those less serious situations—and there are plenty of them—allow for humor. Laugh at it, discuss it if necessary, then move on.

I find that laughter can be one of the best coping mechanisms, but it's important not to confuse having a healthy sense of humor with being immature.

In a power[ed] relationship, there is no room for immaturity. Simply laughing with or at someone does not mean we have a sense of humor. The most distinct difference between immaturity and a healthy sense of humor is that one considers the feelings of others and the other does not. Immaturity frequently finds things funny at the expense of others and is usually accompanied by arrogance. Immaturity laughs at something outside of itself to inflate its own ego while a healthy sense of humor often laughs at itself first—not with self-condemnation, but with a lighthearted ability to see the ironies of life and possibly even learn from them. Immaturity seeks superiority while a sense of humor doesn't seek anything except maybe a good laugh.

If you find it challenging to approach conflict with humor or you struggle to understand why your partner does not see a situation as you do, you might consider the dynamic life system we're a part of. We live in sort of a *Life Soup*.

There are multitudes of life forms—humans, birds, fish, insects, and animals of all sorts. There are human beings in different regions of the world, from different cultures, different races, backgrounds, and speaking different languages. Then there are the different personalities, beliefs, political views, degrees of education, thoughts, and ideas.

These different life systems coexist with varying levels of consciousness and impact on each other and the planet. With such complexities and varieties, we should probably consider it a miracle when our partner agrees with us, or for that matter, anyone. Why are we surprised that it takes some patience, creativity, and humor to get our point across?

But, stir the pot enough and apply the right heat, and you can end up with a delicious meal.

Game time! If you're a couple, grab your playmate and get ready for your next game. *You Gotta Laugh!* If you're single, get ready for your next game *That's Funny!* Both games are about one thing and one thing only—having serious fun!

GAME

You Gotta Laugh!

Rated: MC
Game Rules

Object
To enjoy the power of laughter.

Getting Started
Make time to enjoy activities that make you and you partner laugh.

Here are some suggestions:

- Watching comedy shows (live, movie, or television)
- Dancing
- Singing
- Sharing jokes
- Funny stories or pictures
- Visiting an amusement park, carnival, or fair
- Goofing off at home, the park, other places
- Playing games
- Watching games or sporting events

If you want, list some ideas of your own:

_____

_____

_____

Tip: There are really no requirements for the activities, except they must be activities that make you or you and your partner laugh.

If you do play games, be mindful of whether you or your partner are competitive. This is about laughing, not winning. The sillier the game, the better.

If you and your partner are anything like my husband and me, you may enjoy watching sporting events—but use discretion. This may not make you laugh, particularly if your team loses.

Play the Game
Play whatever activities you and your partner have decided to play. Have fun!

Winning
If you and your partner had fun—you win! Bonus points if your sides hurt from laughing so much!

Challenge
Your partner and you don't enjoy the same things, or they don't want to play this game.

Tip: If your partner does not want to participate or does not have time to play this game, then you play this game yourself. After you have played this game, invite your partner to play another time even if they have shown resistance.

If after three attempts, your partner still refuses to play this game, consider taking a *Time-Out* (refer to Chapter Five). It's likely there are bigger issues standing in the way of your laughing together. If so, these need to be addressed first. Once your issues are addressed, invite your partner to play this game with you.

Regardless of what your partner does, continue to play this game yourself as frequently as you can.

This is not about doing things we like to do or our partner likes to do. It's about laughing. If you and your partner do not laugh at the same things, start off by taking turns. You first. Find things that make you laugh: a funny story, a funny movie, a funny person—and *get your laugh on* first. Then approach your partner about things that make them laugh and let them know you want to have fun with them.

If they accept, enjoy their activity with them and have fun watching them laugh. When the time is right, suggest that you both determine the next fun activity where you can laugh together. Repeat.

END GAME

GAME

Tʜᴀᴛ'ꜱ Fᴜɴɴʏ!

Rated: S
Game Rules

Object
To enjoy the power of laughter (or at least have a smile on your face.)

Getting Started
Make time to enjoy activities that make you laugh or smile. Here are some suggestions: watching comedy shows (live, movie, or TV); reading funny stories; visiting an amusement park, carnival, or fair; dancing; singing; watching games or sporting events. There are no requirements for the activities, except they must make you laugh (or at the very least, smile).

If you want, list some ideas of your own:

_____

_____

_____

_____

Play the Game
Whatever activities you have decided to play, just have fun!

Winning
You have a smile on your face.

Challenge

You don't feel like laughing. Although you may not feel like laughing, still look for things that you find funny. Funny stories, funny pictures, funny movies—just gather your funny stuff together. Wait a day or two, then read, watch, or do whatever you find funny, for at least 10 to 20 minutes. Try doing this every day until you look forward to it. Repeat.

END GAME

Chapter Eight

MC²: Relationship Energy

Energy is everywhere. It sources heat, light, and life. It is utilized by all creatures and appears in different forms. We create an energy in our relationships too. This energy typically develops organically based on the energy of the people and the environment around them. Energy in a relationship can vary from *supportive energy,* in which people listen to and help each other, to *hectic energy,* in which people feel rushed and ignored. Whatever the energy, it permeates throughout the relationship and the entire family. The funny thing about relationship energy is that there's a circular correlation between the relationship energy and the people in the relationship. While relationship energy is generated by the people in the relationship, it then impacts their thoughts, moods, and actions, as well as those of other family members. With that said, doesn't it make sense to actively participate in the creation of that energy instead of letting it randomly develop?

CORE truths, as well as CORE pseudo-truths, create our relationship energy whether we're talking about our relationship at home, at work, or anywhere else. When we tune in to our CORE truths, we can create power[ed] connections. We all have CORE pseudo-truths because we all have fears, insecurities, worries, and concerns. When we pretend CORE pseudo-truths are CORE truths, we end up with pseudo-connections. But when we address our CORE pseudo-truths, our connections, perspectives, and hunches are clearer. Also, our CORE truths can thrive because they are based on knowing ourselves rather than trying to prove something, avoid something, control someone, or manipulate someone.

In a relationship where truth is flipped on and off like a light switch, power^{ed} connections are unlikely to develop. Professing one set of truths to those outside our relationship and a different set of truths to our partner, undoubtedly makes our partner question our sincerity. Sure, we may reserve certain discussions for our partner, but there is no need to tune in to our CORE truths when we are with our partner and tune out when we are with others or vice versa.

The ideal is to cultivate a general appreciation for authenticity and truth. Additionally, a person who accepts and supports the truth of others is better equipped to develop power^{ed} connections with their partner.

Two people who are married or in a committed relationship still need to develop their own support systems to power their own CORE truths. Our partner is in our life to, among many things, support and encourage us, and we, likewise, do the same for them. They contribute to our happiness, but they are not responsible for our happiness. If I feel disconnected or drained, it's not my husband's fault. In fact, it's no one's fault, but it is my responsibility. Sustaining a power^{ed} relationship that powers us and our partner involves developing power^{ed}, authentic relationships with our partner and beyond our partner.

If you have not already, consider joining a community group, social group, or spiritual group that supports your CORE truths. If you are unsure about what group to choose, grab your backpack and try out a few groups until you find ones that fit.

When you and your partner do this together, you create a power^{ed} playground for your relationship. You create a nexus that not only powers you individually but powers you as a couple. A power^{ed} playground with others who share your CORE truths and—even better—augment your CORE truths, allows you and your relationship to increase exponentially and deepens your bond as a couple. Such a playground can become a dynamic power source for your relationship.

My husband and I share support systems. We share the same spiritual community as well as participate in community service work together. We are both members of Agape International Spiritual Center. It is a place where we both feel our CORE truths are well supported. It is also where we met and got married. My husband has a leadership role in one of Agape's community service organizations, in which I am also actively involved. This is part of our power^{ed} playground.

While we do support each other and enjoy sharing our power^{ed} playground, we also have some awesome and inspiring people around us who we play with as well. Teachers, friends, family, mentors, mentees—people we absolutely love—are on our power^{ed} playground. And although our activities sometimes stretch us beyond our comfort zone, participating in these activities and associating with people who inspire and motivate us, powers us. We enjoy our experiences together, and there is a deep sense of satisfaction and connection. Having a power^{ed} playground is essential, whether you are in a committed relationship or not.

What if you and your partner differ regarding what is a suitable support system? What if you don't choose the same power^{ed} playground?

First, don't let this detour either of you. It is important to have support systems that you each are power^{ed} by, so allow each other to explore those places that promote your individual CORE truths. Don't avoid discussions about your choices simply because you choose different support systems. Share your feelings and experiences with each other regarding why these support systems are important to you and how they support your CORE truths. Don't share with the intention of persuading your partner to choose your power^{ed} playground; share with the intention of sharing your CORE truth. Allow yourselves to develop mutual respect for each other's choices and avoid criticisms. Periodically, join your partner on their power^{ed} playground and invite your partner to join you on yours.

Additionally, if your partner or you have a support system of family and friends that recharge your CORE truths, make sure you interact with them regularly and that you reciprocate their support as well. In addition to receiving support, it is equally important that you give support back, particularly to those who support you.

Many of us are associated with business or financial networking groups which are different from what I am referring to here. The primary focus of business networking groups is limited, with the primary focus being financial or business success. Financial and business success are important, and certain networks facilitate our success in these areas. Ideally financial and business successes are just one of the means by which our CORE truths are fulfilled. However, groups and organizations that energize our CORE truths are also important. If you are involved in a business networking group, consider also joining an organization that connects with your CORE truths. Doing so can complement your business networking experience. Again, this applies whether you are already in a relationship or not.

Whenever possible, consider volunteering where you can share your CORE truths. If you are a successful entrepreneur, consider mentoring a young adult. If you are a talented artist, consider volunteering to teach children art. If you love singing, consider joining a choir or singing group. Consider singing groups who visit senior homes and children's hospitals. Whatever you do, connect with your CORE truths while encouraging others to do the same. When you do this as a couple, you increase your experience exponentially and deepen your bond.

Whether through a tweet, instant message, billboard, or commercial, our attention and intention are easily interrupted. Choosing activities and people who recharge us at the CORE truth level is so important. And remember, practicing and respecting our CORE truths impacts our collective human experience, as does *not* practicing and respecting them. The more we collectively honor and connect through our CORE truths, the better experience for ourselves, our partners, our families, and our communities. It improves our collective human network across the planet.

Playgrounds and Playground Etiquette
Most of us know that life is not about playing by ourselves. How ironic it is when we are glued to our electronic devices, ignoring those sitting across the table from us. We live in an era where we have powerful communication devices literally at our fingertips. Sometimes, when we're out to dinner, my husband and I must resist the urge to share thoughts and pictures through our mobile devices. It is obvious we humans are designed to connect with each other and our environment, but let's not forget the people right in front of us.

Also, let's not forget those people we see during our day-to-day activities. We run into them at the store, the bank, the carwash, the gym, a restaurant, school, work, and the metro—literally, everywhere. But have you ever been more captivated by the empty space in front of you, or perhaps even the sidewalk, than by one of these people? Obviously, at work or at school, there are certain manners and protocols we must adhere to, and we should.

But rather than just hurrying through our day, what would happen if we paid a little more attention to others? This is particularly important for those looking for their perfect match. This does not mean we bare our souls to everyone we meet. Nor is this about constructing the best pickup lines or gawking at everyone who passes by. In fact, it is not really about us, per se. But what if we became more mindful of opportunities to share our authentic selves with others and allowed them to do the same?

When the right opportunities appear and we are paying enough attention to take advantage of them, we allow ourselves to connect with others. We're not machines, nor are we in this alone. This simple practice helps us to stay open, rather than closed off. When it comes to our intimate relationship, it's much easier to connect with someone who is power^{ed} than someone whose battery is dead.

But let's be clear—this is not about stroking our ego or creating an outlet for our emotions. Nor is this about being popular or becoming everyone's best friend. This is about authentic, mindful living—not our ego, not our emotions, and not our social calendar (although our social calendar may see a few more entries). Everyone will not agree with or understand our CORE truths. It would be a little suspect if they did. As long as we are respectfully and authentically expressing our CORE truths with no strings attached, I would not be overly concerned. The more we share our CORE truths and encourage others to share theirs, the more connected our lives can become with others, as well as our partner.

We can spend years attempting to perfect an area of our life, yet never feel competent. This occurs when our actions and desired outcomes are not completely in accord. Maybe we like our front yard, but we want flowers. Trimming the bushes and cutting the grass may make our yard look better, but these actions will not produce flowers. If we want flowers, we must find suitable flowers or seeds, plant them, water, and care for them. Being busy is not the same as being productive.

Just doing something does not automatically give us the results we desire. If cultivating your truer self, deepening your connection with your partner, or finding your perfect match are among your goals, make sure your actions are in accordance with those goals by becoming more connected to life, which includes authentically connecting to others.

I cannot emphasize enough how important power^{ed} couples are. Couples have unique opportunities for growth and expansion, as individuals and together, simply because of the unique dynamics within the couple relationship. There are countless opportunities to look at ourselves, our attitudes, and our behaviors, and to improve upon them. Because we share and build a life with our partner, there are incentives to work through situations that may not exist in other relationships. When couples learn to play with these dynamics rather than fight against them, couples become power^{ed} energy sources. As couples become energized, they become energy sources not only for each other, but also for their family, friends, their extended families, and beyond. In a world trying to thrive, power^{ed} couples are invaluable.

Whether you're a power^{ed} couple interested in staying connected or someone looking for your perfect match, it's important to distinguish energy boosters from power drainers. And it's equally important to know how to balance the two. Our final games are about clearly understanding your CORE truths versus CORE pseudo-truths and creating an environment that optimizes your relationship energy.

GAME

Two Naked People: Couples STRIP

Rated: MC
Game Rules

Object

To expose the energy sources or power drainers in your relationship.

Set Up

You will need both of your *Naked Basketball!* SCORE cards from Chapter One and a piece of paper. Remember how, in *Naked Basketball!*, you each stripped? Now you're going to STRIP again but this time you're going to do it a little differently. Now you're going to STRIP together! Also, this game sets you up for your next and final game.

Getting Started

On your SCORE card, look at the type of player you are (in the Team Player Comments column) and your corresponding CORE truth or CORE pseudo-truth (in the STRIP column). Then ask yourselves the questions below, and write down your answers on your piece of paper. BUT BEFORE YOU WRITE DOWN YOUR answers, discuss them with your partner. Start with section S, alternating between you and your partner. Once you've both completed section S, you will then do section C, then O, then R, then E.

Tip

Draw a line to separate section S from section C, and do this for each section—similar to how sections appear on SCORE cards.

You do not have to go over all the CORE truths and CORE pseudo-truths at once. It is perfectly fine to separate them and take a couple days to play this game.

Play the Game

S: SCORE Cards

Get your SCORE cards. Go to Section S and look at the Team Player Comments column and the STRIP column for Player #1.

T: Truth or Pseudo-truth?

Looking at the STRIP column, is this a CORE truth or CORE pseudo-truth? If it's a CORE truth, write it on your piece of paper and put a "T" next to it. If it's a CORE pseudo-truth, write it on your piece of paper and put a "P" next to it.

R: Relationship

What happens in our relationship because I am this, do this, or feel this way? Discuss this with your partner, then write a brief description under the CORE truth or pseudo-truth.

I: Impact

What is the impact on our relationship energy? How does it make our relationship feel? Does it energize our relationship or drain it? Discuss this with your partner. If it energizes the relationship, put an "E" next to your brief description of what happens in the relationship. If it drains the relationship, put a "D" next to it.

P: Power Drainer

What can we do, if anything, to reduce the impact of this power drainer? Discuss this with your partner, then on your paper write what you can do about this power drainer underneath your brief description of what happens in the relationship.

Winning

Easy: if you completed this game, you win!

Challenge

What if you or your partner find this game challenging? That's normal—challenges are part of most games. Or, what if you find someone's CORE truth is a power drainer? Well…

Is it time to take a time-out? Is there any underlying static that needs to be dealt with? Is it time for a little dance lesson? Would a little inspiration help? Keep a sense of humor—don't take yourselves too seriously. It's just a game.

END GAME

GAME

Your Power^{ed} Couple Play

Rated: MC
Game Rules

Object
To boost your energy supply.

Set Up
Now you are two naked people! (I hope you feel sexy.) This final game is about more play—Power^{ed} play! To play this game you will need to refer back to your couple's STRIP answers in *Two Naked People*.

Getting Started
Designate a time period—two or four weeks—to allow enough time to play this game. During this time, you will look for opportunities to boost your relationship energy. Referring to your couple's STRIP paper, you both will look for activities and ways to recharge your relationship, and either convert your power drainers into energy sources, or at least reduce their impact. (Remember, once we address the CORE pseudo-truth, fear, insecurity, or worry, we can discover the CORE truth underneath.)

Play the Game
You and your partner will share ideas and plan events that energize your relationship and reduce power drainers. This includes sharing personal photos, images, messages, and personal notes, as well as sharing ideas for trips, family gatherings, visits with friends, social or community events, concerts, etc. For those who like to create, consider a shared project. Focus on those activities that support the relationship energy

you both want to create. And remember you're doing this naked, so refer back to your couple's STRIP answers as needed.

Your relationship energy impacts not only you and your partner, but those outside of your relationship, too. Your family, friends, and community are all impacted by your relationship energy. Why not consider volunteering together or attending social, spiritual, or political events you are both interested in? And definitely, don't forget about family members. If you have children, definitely include them, too. Help them discover their own CORE truths and their impact on the family dynamic, as appropriate. Also, how about dinner with parents or grandparents, brothers, sisters, and so on. Remember some of the best games are group games, so include others.

Play! Play! Play! Engage in the activities that revive your relationship energy. Stay power^{ed}, playful, and naked.

Winning
This is your Power^{ed} Couple Play. You and your partner decide this one.

END GAME

GAME

Your Power^{ed} Relationship Play

Rated: S
Game Rules

Object
To boost your energy supply.

Set Up
This final game is about more play—Power^{ed} play! To play this game, you will need your *Naked Basketball!* SCORE card from Chapter One. You will refer back to your CORE truths and CORE pseudo-truths in your STRIP column.

Getting Started
In this game, your CORE truths are your energy sources and your CORE pseudo-truths are your power drainers. Designate a time period—one to four weeks—to allow enough time to play this game. During this time, you will explore your relationship energy. You will look for activities and ways to recharge your energy sources, and either convert your power drainers into energy sources, or at least reduce their impact. Remember, once we address the fears, insecurities, worries, etc. related to our CORE pseudo-truths, we can discover our CORE truths.

Play the Game
You will look for ideas and events that energize your relationship energy and reflect your CORE truths. This includes personal photos, images, messages, and personal notes. If you like to create, consider a project that inspires you and reflects your CORE truths. When possible, include ideas for trips, family gatherings, visits with friends,

social or community events, concerts, etc. Focus on those activities that support the relationship energy you want to create.

Put these ideas and plans somewhere you can see them every day—on your phone, computer, poster board—anywhere they'll be visible to you. If it's a personal project(s), not only do you want to make regular time for it, but also create a space(s) to display it that is frequently visible to you.

Remember, your relationship energy impacts anyone you are in a relationship with: your family members, friends, coworkers, and so on. If you have children, definitely include them, too. Help them discover their own CORE truths and their impact on the family dynamic, as appropriate. Also, how about lunch or dinner with parent or grandparent or brother or sister, or friend to boost your relationship energy? Remember, some of the best games are group games, so include others.

Play! Play! Play! Engage in the activities that revive your relationship energy. Stay power^{ed}, playful, and naked.

Winning
This is your Power^{ed} Relationship Play, so I'll let you decide this one.

Challenge
Do you find this game challenging? That's normal—challenges are part of most games.

Is there someone you need to take a time-out with? Is there any underlying static that needs to be dealt with? Is there someone you find challenging whom you need to know better? Is your backpack ready? Keep a sense of humor—don't take yourself too seriously. It's just a game.

END GAME

Power^ed Play is about more than being a couple or finding our perfect match. It's about recognizing and understanding what <u>C</u>reates <u>O</u>ur <u>R</u>elationship <u>E</u>nergy—our own and those we are connecting with. It's about connecting, not only with our spouse or significant other but also other family members, relatives, friends, neighbors, communities, and beyond. It's about understanding that how we do or don't connect with those closest to us is likely to be reflected in how we will or won't connect to those not close to us. And connections based on fears, secrets or worries created distorted or pseudo-connections. Additionally, Power^ed Play is about figuring out how to handle broken connections, so they don't drain us and how to recharge those energy sources that help our relationships thrive. It's about recognizing our CORE truths, even our CORE pseudo-truths, and knowing the difference as well as going beyond the superficial or external to really see another person's CORE truths and possibly understand their CORE pseudo-truths. It's about creating connected people to create a power^ed world because in this world, every connection counts.

About the Author

Gail A. W. Silverstein shares details about her life in this book. This book is her labor of love and service. She sincerely hopes you find it helpful, fun, and worthy of sharing with family and friends. If you have questions or would like to connect with her and keep informed regarding relationship activities, please email her at: nakedbasketball@gmail.com.

www.ingramcontent.com/pod-product-compliance
Lightning Source LLC
Chambersburg PA
CBHW072146160426
43197CB00012B/2273